Guiding Curriculum Development

Other Titles by This Author

Competency-Based Leadership: A Guide for High Performance in the Role of the School Principal (R&L Education, July 2013)

Human Resources Function in School Districts (Rowman & Littlefield Publishers, December 1999)

The Changing Landscape of School Leadership: Recalibrating the School Principalship (Rowman & Littlefield Publishers, December 2015)

The Legal World of the School Principal: What Leaders Need to Know about School Law (Rowman & Littlefield Publishers, May 2016)

The Principal as a Learning-Leader: Motivating Students by Emphasizing Achievement (R&L Education, November 2012)

Guiding Curriculum Development

The Need to Return to Local Control

M. Scott Norton

ROWMAN & LITTLEFIELD
Lanham • Boulder • New York • London

Published by Rowman & Littlefield
A wholly owned subsidiary of The Rowman & Littlefield Publishing Group, Inc.
4501 Forbes Boulevard, Suite 200, Lanham, Maryland 20706
www.rowman.com

Unit A, Whitacre Mews, 26-34 Stannary Street, London SE11 4AB

Copyright © 2016 by M. Scott Norton

All rights reserved. No part of this book may be reproduced in any form or by any electronic or mechanical means, including information storage and retrieval systems, without written permission from the publisher, except by a reviewer who may quote passages in a review.

British Library Cataloguing in Publication Information Available

Library of Congress Cataloging-in-Publication Data

Names: Norton, M. Scott, author.
Title: Guiding curriculum development : the need to return to local control / M. Scott Norton.
Description: Lanham : Rowman & Littlefield, a wholly owned subsidiary of The Rowman & Littlefield Publishing Group, Inc., [2016] | Includes bibliographical references and index.
Identifiers: LCCN 2016023168 (print) | LCCN 2016030908 (ebook) | ISBN 9781475827989 (cloth : alk. paper) | ISBN 9781475827996 (pbk. : alk. paper) | ISBN 9781475828009 (Electronic)
Subjects: LCSH: Curriculum planning—United States. | School boards—United States—Decision making. | Schools—Decentralization—United States
Classification: LCC LB2806.15 .N67 2016 (print) | LCC LB2806.15 (ebook) | DDC 375/.001—dc23
LC record available at https://lccn.loc.gov/2016023168

∞ ™ The paper used in this publication meets the minimum requirements of American National Standard for Information Sciences Permanence of Paper for Printed Library Materials, ANSI/NISO Z39.48-1992.

Printed in the United States of America

Contents

Preface	vii
Chapter 1: Curriculum's Missing Link: The Need to Return to Local Control	1
Chapter 2: Foundations of Supervision and Curriculum Development in America	25
Chapter 3: Teaching and Learning: Promoting Student Achievement	49
Chapter 4: Determining Learning Standards	69
Chapter 5: The School's Curriculum: Local, State, or Federal?	89
Chapter 6: Supervision: Improving Classroom Teaching	111
Chapter 7: Organizing for Curriculum Evaluation and Assessment	135
Index	151
About the Author	159

Preface

The primary focus of the book is to provide a guide for school leaders at the local school level for taking the leadership for the planning, designing, implementing, evaluating, and assessing of school curriculum, and establishing effective related supervisory practices. What is being taught in the nation's classrooms looms of most importance to the nation's future. Historically, education has been viewed as a local function. That is, states were to establish the guiding goals and objectives for educational programs and the local school district was to have local administrators determine how best to meet student needs and implement a learning program that served those needs. Yet contemporary practices regarding the federal government's mandates as to what is taught in the schools and how it is taught have inhibited the ability of local schools to plan and implement curricular provisions in the best interests and needs of children and youth. It is not that federal agencies should not have a concern for the effectiveness of education, but such concern should be demonstrated in terms of national support as opposed to local control.

At present, recent legislative actions at the federal level give some hope that educational decisions can be returned to the various states and local school communities. The passing of the legislation Every Child Succeeds Act could well lead to more authority for local schools to decide what learners should know and be able to do. If, however, increased local control of curricular provisions is given to school communities in the United States, school principals and other administrative leaders logically must be prepared to actually assume the leadership for the processes of planning, development, and evaluation of the curriculum. School principals, themselves, have expressed doubts about their preparedness to assume such important administrative roles. Administrator preparation programs have not given high priority to curriculum development and the process activities involved are complex and often controversial. Administrator in-service activities necessarily will have to gear up in this area to bring about the needed professional development of paramount importance for curricular programming.

This book will help aspiring school principals, assistant principals, central office administrators, and other education preparation personnel to understand and meet the curriculum and supervision demands of today by

- Underscoring the changing purposes of supervisory practices and curricular development in education; by identifying the issues/problems related to federal intervention in curriculum matters at the local school level; and by supporting the need to return educational matters to local control of education in the United States.
- Gaining a knowledge of the historical research findings and empirical evidence relating to human motivation, leadership effectiveness, human relations, and administrative supervision that has served as the foundation of effective contemporary practices in education.
- Discussing how humans learn and the many factors and conditions that influence effective or ineffective teaching and learning results for students.
- Examining standards-based learning in relation to its surrounding controversies and probable future.
- Illustrating the varying concepts of educational curriculum and supporting the view of local control of teaching and learning to meet the interests and needs of students.
- Viewing the school principal as an effective instructional program supervisor.
- Examining the related concepts of curriculum evaluation/assessment and the benefits related to student learning.

THE ORGANIZATION OF THE BOOK

The book has seven chapters that are focused on these specific purposes. The book is "reader friendly" and written so as to engage the reader into each chapter by using such strategies as pre-quizzes with follow-up research information, inserting "snapshots" and "stories" to illustrate the effectiveness of various administrative practices, using discussion questions to extend the reader's understanding of chapter concepts, presenting case studies that place the reader in the role of school leader, and listing follow-up references for instructional purposes.

Although the school principal and other school leaders' hands are often tied by such factors as state and federal mandates, lack of sufficient resources, high teacher turnover, high-stakes testing demands, and constant changes in curricular programming requirements, the book places emphasis on administrative personnel for increasing their knowledge and skill of curriculum and supervision practices toward the goals of effective administrative provisions in the major role of schools today—the effective planning, designing, implementing, and evaluating of the curriculum for the benefit of student learners.

Chapter 1

Curriculum's Missing Link

The Need to Return to Local Control

Primary chapter goal: To underscore the changing purposes of supervisory practices in education, to identify the issues/problems related to federal intervention in curriculum matters at the local school level, and to support the need to return educational matters to a local function of public school education in the United States.

EDUCATIONAL SUPERVISION AND CURRICULUM DEVELOPMENT

An Overview of Purpose

The question regarding just what student learning experiences should be provided for all students remains controversial throughout the various states and federal offices. Historically, education has been considered a national concern, state responsibility, and local function. That is, the U.S. Constitution gave the states and the people the authority to establish the guiding goals and objectives of educational programs and school districts were delegated the authority to determine just how to meet student needs.

As time has passed, the federal government's concerns have become closer to mandates. Contemporary federal involvement has risen to the level of controlling the curriculum of local schools with a provision that failure to follow the mandated core curriculum would result in a restriction of federal fund entitlements. In some instances, mandated curriculum has set forth what the teacher is to teach and just how it is to be taught. As underscored by Berlak (2003),

> As a nation we will continue to differ profoundly on how schools ought to educate, what educated persons ought to know and how best to teach the young to read. In a democracy we cannot allow federal and state officials, government appointed boards and panels of experts remote from communities, classrooms and students to make these choices and thereby control our school's curriculum and our children's future. (p. 7)

Much has been written regarding the pros and cons of federal and state control of educational programming. Margaret I. Haddermann (1988) identified various advantages and disadvantages of increased state and federal control of local school curricula. For example, advantages of such control include benefits for disadvantaged groups such as special needs children and youth, reduction in the disparities among the states and their ability to tax and pay for educational expenditures, and provisions to bridge the gap among school districts relative to both quantity and quality of program offerings.

The disadvantages of tighter external controls include the fact that most significant program improvements occur when local schools are given the responsibility to determine program decisions, the fact that underfunded and unfunded state and federal mandates have not shown the expected improvements, and the fact that handed-down program mandates are often contrary to local school goals and needs and to fostering social independence and program creativity. In addition, constant changes in program requirements tend to result in confused leadership and a reluctance for highly qualified school personnel to enter or remain in the profession; student achievement is actually inhibited rather than facilitated.

As emphasized by Haddermann (1988), nearly thirty years ago, "The new state primacy is a drastic reversal of American political ideology, which has traditionally spurned distant government in favor of decision-making power closer to home. To assure balance, states can avoid prescribing the details of school practice and school boards can assert their leadership role" (p. 1).

In any case, school boards must give serious attention to their policy-making responsibility that sets forth what the school programs are to achieve. In turn, school superintendents and the professional staff must assume the responsibility for drafting viable administrative regulations that establish how the board's policies will be implemented and accounted. The push for increasing intervention of federal government into state and local education programming must end. A return to local autonomy at the state and local levels is essential. There is no role for the federal government in setting local school program standards. State and local authorities must take charge of their own accountability regarding the proper learning standards for school programs. Chapter 4 discusses this matter in further detail.

Few people would argue against the principle that effective instruction should be designed and implemented to meet a student's personal interests and needs. Empirical and basic research evidence make it clear that students are different—different in intellectual ability and the ability to achieve academically. Yet, most federal and state standards establish the achievement levels that all students must reach at each grade level. The graded system of school organization remains in place; the student commonly has to pass the standard score for grade 3, for example, before being passed to grade 4. Moving children ahead with their peers is not the negative implication of social promotion; rather it is moving them ahead according to their success level of learning and achievement at a place and time in their developing lives.

Research studies have made it clear that students in grade 3 and of ages eight to nine commonly will achieve varying reading scores from grades 1 and 2 to grades 4 through 7. The practice is similar to setting a high jump standard for all grade 3 students at 3 1/2 feet. Some students will clear the jump the first try and some will never clear that height as a third grader.

Schools in the United States have moved closer to having a national curriculum, although several states have refused to accept or have withdrawn from the recent federal mandated Common Core curriculum. This book, however, is founded on the concept of a "local function of education" and places the processes of curriculum planning, organization, implementation, and assessment under the control of local schools and the leadership of the school principal and professional staff. Effective curriculum programs are contingent on several factors including the determination of the educational interests and needs of students, the formulation of relevant program goals, the establishment of appropriate educational objectives, the determination of individualized learning standards, the provision of group and individual learning experiences, the setting of strategies for curriculum evaluation and assessment, and the programming of changes/improvements in curricular offerings and teaching methods.

Top-down mandates leave no room for creativity and inhibit program commitment. Yet school principals and the professional staff are held accountable for student achievement results. Both parties have expressed the willingness to be held accountable for student achievement results if given the authority to determine what program strategies are best suited for achieving individual student goals.

LOCAL CONTROL—THE TIME IS RIGHT

Nearly two decades ago, Ravitch and Viteritti (1997) pointed out the inhibiting factors of an externally mandated and controlled school curriculum. These authorities made note of the spectacular curriculum results that can be accomplished by the sharing of power of the central administration and the local schools. What prohibits the effectiveness of school leaders and teachers to employ such positive results? According to Ravitch and Viteritti, the answer to the question is as follows:

> A school system that seeks to restrict initiative by imposing an elaborate command-and-control mechanism, that attempts to manage all of its employees through uniform and burdensome mandates and regulation, that stamps out efforts to find a different (perhaps better) way of educating children, and that lacks meaningful standards for what children should learn but has elaborate standards for the delivery of mediocre services. (p. 4)

Headlines in the *Arizona Republic* read, "Congress Votes to Repeal No Child Left Behind Law" (Theobald & Troyan, 2015, p. 1A). The Senate voted to send a bill to the president of the United States that overhauls federal K–12 education policy and ends more than a decade of strict federal control over schools. Arizona senator John McCain was quoted as saying, "This legislation is a major step forward in getting Washington out of Arizona's classrooms and putting states, teachers, and parents back in charge of educating our students" (Theobald & Troyan, p. 14A).

Education leaders and other state and local individuals viewed the new legislation, termed the Every Student Succeeds Act, in a favorable manner. Indeed, every learner should be able to advance in relation to his or her potential. For example, one school superintendent commented that the new aforementioned legislation would move schools away from the current one-size-fits-all approach and restore education decision making to those who know our schools best. Other notables mentioned the new legislation's benefits as having more control coming back to the local schools, allowing states to address its special needs and achievement gaps, reducing Washington's role in setting academic standards and penalizing schools for missing achievement gaps, changing the top-down approach that ties the hands of teachers and local school administrators, and moving schools away from the "no-child-left-untested" law.

Some cautions were set forth by some individuals regarding the new Every Student Succeeds Act. For example, conservatives are concerned that the new law will still retain too much control. Others objected to the removal of the provision that would allow parents to opt out of having their children take standardized tests, and some people stated that the challenge was to make sure that the new law does not result in having the state replace the federal government in overreaching its role in educational policy. That is, local control of school programming must be assured. In any case, the new law, if signed into practice, will set the stage for accomplishing the needed opportunities for local school districts and schools to take the leadership in determining the educational curriculum for students.

The need for present and future school principals to be prepared to assume the leadership for local school curriculum development is essential. However, it is questionable at this time as to whether practicing principals are indeed knowledgeable and sufficiently skilled to take over such responsibilities. An examination of the courses of study at administrator preparation institutions for prospective school leaders reveals that little attention is given to curriculum development.

We asked several school principals what curriculum program implementations they would change or initiate if they were given the authority to do so. Their common reaction was, after a long pause, that they were not really certain what they would do. In any case, the new law, if enacted into law, would set the stage for local school districts and schools to take the leadership in determining the educational curriculum for students.

Of most importance is that the school principal realizes that he or she has become a key component for curriculum development in the school. School principals nationally have made it clear that the current nine-month work schedule for teachers does not allow enough time to do the job expected of them. A twelve-month work schedule for administrators and other school employees must become the next innovation for school districts nationally. Time is needed for the development of a total learning culture within the school district and school community. Respect for the teaching profession must become more than a hopeful plea. This does not infer a twelve-month school year for students. The focus is on professional development and planning time for curriculum improvement.

Most any effective teacher can find challenging positions outside education and for a much higher salary. The myth that administrators and teachers do the work just because they love kids is flawed. Teachers must be student advocates, but salary rewards are normal concerns for educators as well. In addition, the engagement of parents into their child's education remains important. Research results have made it clear that when parents are involved in partnerships with schools and school leaders in support of their children positive educational outcomes result.

AN EFFECTIVE SCHOOL CURRICULUM REQUIRES COMPETENT SUPERVISION

A common definition of the term *supervision* is how school personnel use adults for the purpose of maintaining school operations to influence the attainment of major goals and objectives necessary for optimal student learning. Curriculum and supervision are inextricably related. Supervisory practices do change with the ever-flowing needs of a changing society. Nevertheless, each historical phase of supervisory concepts leaves its imprint on contemporary practices. A knowledge of the history of supervision is needed for an understanding and appreciation of recommended current practices. Best research results in medicine or best practices in any professional field serve foundationally to support current practice and as a basis for extending further research. For these reasons, we discuss the evolution of supervision in the following sections of this chapter.

Evolution of Supervision

As noted by Finch and Crunkilton (2015), "Curriculum as we know it today has evolved over the years from a narrow set of disjointed offerings to a comprehensive array of relevant student learning experiences" (p. 1). Early methods of supervision in schools were tied to Frederick Taylor's (1911) concepts of scientific management. The division of labor, technical supervision, specific rules/procedures to follow, and other machine-like practices were implemented first in business and industry.

The revolutionary scientific practices were so successful for increasing production that education was quick to jump on the bandwagon and adopt scientific management concepts as well. In education, the school leader's responsibility was to set forth the procedures to be followed by the teacher and the teacher's responsibility was to carry them out. Professional education conferences at the time included presentations on how to teach music scientifically and how to present all subjects using scientific methodology.

School administrators were anxious to implement the scientific management concept, and teachers were not reluctant to participate in this manner primarily because they were actually unprepared to do otherwise. The school district leader was to serve as the district's CEO, an impressive new title for a school superintendent. Many teachers at the elementary school level in the early 1900s had just graduated from high school, and it was only later in history that the two-year normal school gave potential teachers some instruction in the principles of teaching, use of teaching materials, and other information related to instruction in the classroom.

The recommended methods for supervisory practices have been identified in various sources throughout history. The following section sets forth the primary supervisory themes of educational supervision historically. The descriptions are only excerpts of supervisory and curriculum administrative practices of the time. The practices at the time of their influence were much more complex and controversial than set forth briefly as follows.

Historical Perspectives of Supervision and Curriculum Provisions

During colonial times, local initiatives established the parochial and public schools that were governed by community influentials termed *selectmen*.

These select committees closely supervised the school program and determined just what the hired teacher was to teach. Selectmen commonly had limited knowledge themselves about the processes of teaching and learning but made sure that certain religious principles were instilled in the minds of the children and youth. Reading was stressed in the early ages of a child's schooling so that students could study the Bible.

Teacher institutes were slowly established for giving teachers lessons in the teaching of reading, arithmetic, use of globes, and "school keeping." Bloss (1882), Indiana's superintendent of public instruction, noted in his annual report the vital importance of the county institute for teachers. He pointed out that the teacher institutes were essential for improving the work of teachers and enabling them to compare their methods with those of other teachers. The normal two-year school for teacher preparation became fully established within the states by the middle of the nineteenth century. Progressive education loomed important; learning by doing, importance of the arts, and individualism of instruction became dominant and continued to influence classroom practices for decades to come.

1900–1920

Early methods of supervision continued ties to Taylor's ideas of scientific supervision, procedural controls, and scientific management. The scientific management methods were readily accepted because they were especially effective in industry; production was greatly increased. The select committees that micromanaged the programs of the school ultimately evolved into school boards as we know them today.

1920–1930

Highly controlled supervision continued in the form of elected community school boards and authoritative school superintendents and school masters. Teachers with four-year teacher preparation programs were few and far between. School principals were comprised commonly of experienced teachers that had performed in the role of teacher in a superior fashion, although many elementary, junior high, and high school principals also taught part-time, especially at the elementary school level.

1930–1945

The expansion of population and the need for more city schools were accompanied by growth awareness of human development and the importance of education for the continuation of a democratic nation. Democratic supervision came to the forefront. The work of many individuals including Mary Parker Follett (1924) established the vital importance of recognizing the human factor in an organization. Parker's concepts of coordination were instrumental in reinforcing methods of supervisory and personnel practices in all organizations. In addition, Lewin, Lippitt, and White (1939) conducted research that revealed that a democratic leadership style resulted in more positive learning for students than authoritarian or laissez-faire leadership styles. During this time period democratic methods dominated the thinking of educational personnel. Democratic supervision, democratic teaching, democratic administration, and democratic relationships were the popular things to do. Central office curriculum administrators were commonly given the title of coordinator rather than the more controlling title of director. By 1944, there was a push toward educating the majority of students for employment in the real world, whereas other students were prepared for the more advanced college courses.

1945–1955

The components of supervision must include administration of goals and standards, as well as instruction based on delivery methods, community needs, and in-service development programs. Supervision as curriculum implementation focused on the concept that supervision must find its meaning in curriculum development. Technical supervision included planning and organization; these administrative processes related to how administrators must adapt to the symptoms of societal change. Supervision and curriculum development were to result in positive change. The literature was replete with criticism of the failure of the educational system in the United States. Schools were viewed as education's wasteland, a land of mediocrity and a reason to be feared because of the "superiority" of science advancements by the Soviet Union (Owens, 2001).

1955–1965

The dimensions of supervision must include the administration of goals and objectives as well as instruction based on delivery methods, community needs, and in-service development programs. Supervision as curriculum implementation continued to focus on the concept that supervision must find its meaning in curriculum development. The dimensions of supervision must include the administration of purpose, goals, and standards as well as instruction based on delivery methods, community needs, and continuous professional growth. In 1957, the event of Sputnik by the Soviet Union led to a new federal program titled No Child Left Behind. New federal controls were established for education in the special areas of science, mathematics, and foreign language. Expansion called for new personnel specializations. Sputnik, influences of world conflicts, and new views of pedagogy brought about the need for new thinking about what was to be taught, the standards to be achieved academically by students, and the new knowledge and skills that had to be accomplished to meet societal needs. Criticism of the conservative views of education was prominent and progressiveness once again was promoted to bring educational practices back to life.

1965–1975

Models for comprehensive programs of supervision were established. For example, clinical supervision models loomed important for improving individual teacher performances. Clinical supervision emphasized systemwide instructional improvement through improved staff performance. Emphasis was placed on supervisor and teacher cooperative relationships.

1975–1985

Supervision came about as the need for ongoing evaluation and assessment of teaching performance. Program goals and objectives served as the guides for instructional services by school district administrators. Both the states and federal government assumed more control of program offerings at the local school level. Federal monies were accompanied by mandates relative to programs and services rendered. Student achievement standards were to be implemented, tested, and assessed. Teacher evaluations were mandated. School principals commonly were spending one-third of their time completing teacher performance evaluations. Such publications as *A Nation at Risk* underscored the contention that education in the United States was seriously inferior to that of the Soviet Union and other countries of the world.

1985–1995

The importance of the school principal as an instructional leader became increasingly important as opposed to being a "maintenance" administrator. Performance evaluations for teachers continued. Student high-stakes testing became prominent and more problematic for school leaders. Educational goals and objectives began to include more attention to achievement standards. Although the criticism of education in the United States continued, respectable scholars directly rebutted the "myths" purposely manufactured by people that were promoting fraudulent information about the status of education in the United States with publications such as Berliner and Biddle's *The Manufactured Crisis: Myths, Fraud, and the Attack on America's Public Schools* (1995).

1995–2005

Supervision as collaborative leadership is practiced. Models of leadership became prominent in the preparation programs of school administration. The

Interstate School Leaders Licensure Consortium (ISLLC) Standards set forth by the ISLLC captured the attention of higher education preparation programs for school principals and district office administrators. Of the six major standards set forth by ISLLC, four of the standards held primary implications for administrative leadership in the areas of curriculum, instruction, and supervision in local schools. Administrators as learning leaders was featured. The federal legislation of the No Child Left Behind Act of 2001 was revolutionary. It represented a major takeover of program offerings at the local school level. Its major "control" of educational curriculum and practices was to continue for the better part of two decades. The concept of establishing educational standards for students' education became a reality primarily as a result of a series of educational summit meetings that included high-level representatives of government and corporation executives.

2005–2015

The continuation of improving student achievement and meeting the special needs of all children and youth was the focus of supervisory practices during this time period. The principal as a learning leader was of the most importance. Mandated student high-stakes testing was prevalent throughout the states. Toward the end of 2015, some states were of the opinion that school programs should give less time to testing and more time to classroom learning. School principals, although heavily involved in the teacher evaluation process, were being encouraged to serve more assertively as coaches and mentors for gaining instructional improvement. Teacher turnover continued as problematic. Quality teachers were leaving the profession at high percentages.

2015–Present

Core curriculum programs set forth by the federal government and adopted by many states were topics of controversy and disagreement. Although not universal by any means, authorities in education and other roles were calling for a needed return to local control. Top-down curricular mandates were evidenced in core curriculum programs set forth by the federal and state governments of several states. The concept that local school boards, school administrative leaders, and community patrons were in the best position to determine school curriculum and instructional methods to meet student interests and needs crept slowly back into contention. Because local schools work within the school system, the articulation of program provisions within each grade level was given priority; content remained important. Although not signed by the president of the United States at the time of this writing, the Every Student Succeeds Act passed by Congress reportedly was to have a major influence on returning the control of curricular offerings back to the states and the local school districts.

The School Principal as an Effective Supervisor

Definitions of the term *supervision* are influenced by the social and economic conditions of the time in which they are formed. The common definition of supervision is how school principals use adults for the purpose of maintaining and changing the operations of the school to directly influence the attainment of major instructional goals and objectives of the school's program. A closely related view of supervision is action and experimentation implemented for the purpose of improving instruction and the curricular program. That is, supervision finds its meaning in the school curriculum. It is through intelligent supervisory practices that the school principal demonstrates his or her talents as a learning leader, a student advocate, and a human resources administrator. What about administrator preparation? Are college/university preparation programs capable of meeting curricular demands?

The historic and contemporary issues surrounding curricular practices include questions related to the mission of the public school, its primary purposes. Originating purposes centered on religious rationale. Today, religion can play no part in public schools. The scope of the curriculum is a continuing issue. Is the scope to be centered on vocational outcomes or is college preparation its primary focus? What about the issue of leadership? Is supervision based on the term's etymology whereby the prefix *super* means "over" and the suffix *vision* means "to see" (i.e., to oversee). Or should the word be defined in terms of support and improvement?

Another curricular issue is that of public involvement. To what extent must parents be involved in the design and implementation of the school's curriculum? To what extent is curriculum a local function? Other issues such as private compared with public schools, federal mandates compared with local autonomy, and free public education kindergarten through college have come to the fore as a contemporary curricular issue. At this time in history, vouchers, whereby parents can send their child to any public or private school, once again have come into play.

In summary, testing issues (What? How much? What kind?), class size and achievement, grouping and placement, special needs programs, gifted programs, health and sex education, language usage, student retention, acceleration, grading, cultural bias, punitive discipline, compensatory programs, outcomes-based education, nongraded elementary school programs, home schooling, core curriculum, and other issues are among those troublesome issues faced in our schools today.

Dimensions of supervision include these constructs:

1. Administration—The establishment of educational goals and standards; asserting the needed leadership for achieving stated goals; communicating the vision and mission of the school; planning, organizing, and implementing the school's curriculum; staffing, motivating, developing, and evaluating staff performance and goal attainment; and leading the development of a learning culture in the school.
2. Curriculum—Evaluating and assessing the curriculum gaps between achievement results and expectations; reviewing the school's vision and mission statements and making appropriate additions or changes as fits the case; designing and implementing the school's curriculum according to student needs and interests, the vision and mission, special student services, available resources and materials, school facilities, necessary expenditures, appropriate staff development, and effective staff collaboration; and implementing the program(s) as now determined.
3. Instruction—Curriculum implemented within the classrooms; supervisory mentoring, supporting, evaluating, accounting, and procedures for retaining staff talent implemented.

What Are the Bases of Supervision?

The knowledge and skill bases for school leaders relative to effective supervisory practices include collaboration, communication, observing, coaching, planning, organizing, conferencing, supporting, problem solving, researching, and improving human resources.

In accomplishing the knowledge and skills required for effective supervision, several key administrative competencies are as follows:

1. Understanding that schools are people; schools progress as people grow and develop.
2. Being highly competent as a curriculum developer.
3. Being highly competent as an instructional specialist; student learning is foremost.
4. Being highly competent in human relations; supervision is a cooperative process.
5. Understanding and practicing effective skills required of a coach and mentor. Staff development is important.
6. Understanding that administrative tasks are symptoms of change that must be resolved.
7. Realizing that change is ongoing and requires the development of new administrative knowledge and skills.
8. Being highly competent in the evaluation and assessment of curriculum improvement.

9. Being able to work faster than a speeding bullet, able to solve big problems in a single day, and being more powerful than a locomotive to stop decreases in educational funding.

AN OVERVIEW OF THE SCHOOL'S CURRICULUM

The Tenth Amendment of the U.S. Constitution states that the powers not granted to the United States are reserved to the states or to the people. This book's purposes center on the need for placing the responsibility for determining student curriculum and academic achievement at the local school level whereby school personnel determine the individual student's personal interests and needs. In turn, an individual curricular program for each student is designed, approved, and implemented. Presently, teachers are inhibited in their ability to teach effectively and students are not reaching their full learning potential. That is, the creativity of teachers is inhibited in attempts to implement top-down academic standards and instructional methods viewed as effective by "experts" at the national level.

If instruction is to be designed to meet the individual interests and needs of the learner, who is in the best position to determine such needs? We submit that the social, mental, and physical needs of children and youth are determined best by local educational professionals. Such professionals include local central office personnel, school principals, and classroom teachers. Local control opens the door of opportunity for greater parental involvement and influence on educational matters as well.

The current trend toward a national curriculum over time is likely to end. The questions that need to be answered are: Are the local school educators prepared to assume the leadership responsibilities for curriculum development? Are the current administrator preparation programs preparing potential school principals to assume this task? Are the current professional development programs for practicing school principals focusing on the complex task of curriculum development?

In recent surveys of school principals' current position responsibilities, the task of curriculum development commonly is not mentioned. This fact is understandable in view of the current top-down core programs being mandated by federal agencies. In one instance, school principals were asked the question, "If the local function for building and implementing school curriculum were given to you by legislative and school board actions, what would you change or do?" The common answer was, "I really am not sure."

School leaders must be prepared to plan, organize, implement, and assess an effective curriculum program for their school. As stated by Abbott (2014),

> The concept of local control is grounded in a philosophy of government premised on the belief that the individuals and institutions closest to the students

and most knowledgeable about a school—and most invested in the welfare and success of its educators, students, and communities—are best suited to making important decisions related to its operation, leadership, staffing, academics, teaching, and improvement. (p. 1)

As noted by Haddermann as early as 1988,

The new state primacy is a drastic reversal of American political ideology, which has traditionally spurned distant government in favor of decision-making power close to home. To restore balance, states can avoid over prescribing the details of school practice, and school boards can assert their leadership role. (p. 1)

Everyone knows the meaning of school curriculum or do they? The following pre-quiz asks ten questions about school curriculum. Each question is either true or false. Do not just guess the answer. If you do not know the answer, just skip the question and go on to the next question. Check your score at the end of the exercise.

Pre-Quiz on School Curriculum

1. The term *curriculum* is of Greek derivation meaning "to study broadly." True____ or False____
2. Today, the term *curriculum* has been clarified by the courts and means a school's requirements for graduation. True____ or False____
3. Recent congressional action has placed the jurisdiction for curriculum solely within the control of the local school district. True____ or False____
4. The concept of local control is based on the belief that the people and school districts closest to the students are in the best position to know the best educational interests and needs of children and youth. True____ or False____
5. The U.S. Congress recently passed a bill that establishes the right of teachers to decide what is to be taught in their subject(s) and the instructional methods to be used in teaching the subject. True____ or False____
6. Curriculum is the foundation on which the practice of supervision rests. True____ or False____
7. Because the philosophy that dominates the meaning of the term *curriculum* differs among the states and individuals within the states, it is virtually impossible for school districts to take actions leading to school improvement. True____ or False____
8. Although school principals must be knowledgeable of what learning experiences are being provided for students in their schools, the cur-

ricular program for schools and the specifics regarding topics of study in each subject must be determined by the school board that has been delegated this task by the state legislature. True____ or False____
9. Teacher autonomy is based on the philosophy that the teacher has the authority to decide what is to be taught to students in a specific course being offered. True____ or False____
10. A common definition of the term *curriculum* is that it represents a vast array of learning activities and experiences provided by the school for purposes of student learning. True____ or False____

Answers: 1. F; 2. F; 3. F; 4. T; 5. F; 6. T; 7. F; 8. T; 9. F; 10. T.
Your Score

10–9 correct: You receive 5 stars
8–7 correct: You receive 4 stars
6–5 correct: You receive 3 stars
4–3 correct: You receive 2 stars
2–1 correct: You receive 1 star
0 correct: Sorry, we are out of stars

A Discussion of Answers to the Pre-Quiz

1. Question 1 is false. The term *curriculum* is not of Greek derivation. Rather, curriculum is from the Latin word *currere*, meaning to "run the course" (Wiles & Bondi, 1996). This meaning ultimately led to the contemporary understanding of curriculum as the course of study or learning path. Historically definitions and understandings of the term have been more similar than different. For example, nearly one hundred years ago Bobbitt (1918) stated that curriculum was those things that pupils must learn to deal with in the race of life.

   An early 1951 textbook defined curriculum similarly as all the activities and learning experiences of students that are carried forward under the direction of the teachers (Spears, 1951). McNeil (2003) attempted to view curriculum from the vantage points of one's position and role. For example, he contended that policy makers tend to view curriculum in terms of standards and achievement, school administrators view curriculum as the school's educational program, teachers see the term as what they hope students will learn, and publishers and specialists in the academic field view it as packages of instructional material such as texts and instructional resources.

   Marsh and Willis (2003) set forth eight different definitions of curriculum before selecting their working definition of the term as follows: "Curriculum is an interrelated set of plans and experiences that a student undertakes under the guidance of the school" (p. 13). This definition is sufficient for the purposes of this book. However, we would prefer to insert the word *learning* before the word *plans* in the preceding definition.

2. Question 2 is false. There has been no action by the courts that specifically defines the term *curriculum*. As stated in the answer to Question 1, the term commonly is defined as what educational experiences are offered students in school programs for the purpose of learning. It is of interest to note, however, that court cases have decided on some cases when an individual sued the school district for not giving them an adequate education. For example, a student filed a lawsuit alleging that his lack of gaining an education was as a result of malpractice of the school officials and the failure of teachers to perform their duties and obligations sufficiently. The student sought a claim of $5 million. The appellant court ruled against the claim, stating that such judgments about the past would require a daily review of occurrences and school practices (*Donahue v. Copiague* USFD, N.Y. 2nd 440, NY Court of Appeals (1979)-Ed. Malpractice).

3. Question 3 is false. No legal action to place authority for curriculum decisions solely in the hand of local school districts has ever been taken. Only recently, however, the U.S. Congress passed a bill that gives local school boards more authority regarding curricular program decisions. At the time of this writing, this legislation, Success for Every Student, was awaiting the signature of the president of the United States. This action serves the purposes of this book in a most positive way.

4. Question 4 is true. The primary rationale, underlying local control is the contention that such authority gives curricular decisions to those educators closest to the personal needs and interests of the learners. As previously stated in this chapter, local school districts are more prepared to know and understand the culture of their school community and thus able to address the educational issues and problems encountered in an expedient, creative manner. As noted by Abbott (2014), increasing local control can serve to improve academic quality and teaching effectiveness; increase local pride, civic participation, and public financial support; and improve teaching and student performance.

5. Question 5 is false. Legislation to give a teacher authority to determine his or her own curriculum has never been considered from a legal standpoint. From a legal perspective, the authority for educational policy decisions is delegated to the local school board by the state. In turn, the school board delegates the process of developing administrative procedures for implementing the school policies. Schools are

"systems" and require a coordinated program of student studies. Just give thought to the chaos that would result if every teacher taught only what he or she wanted to teach. Curriculum development is a planned and organized school system matter. Autonomy is given to teachers in relation to their methods of instruction and creative abilities.
6. Question 6 is true. Supervision finds its meaning in curriculum. Supervision is action and experimentation aimed at improving instruction and the curricular program. Curriculum, instruction, and administration are inextricably related. Administration centers on such processes as planning, organization, staffing, coordination, communication, and budgeting. Curriculum includes dimensions such as program goals and objectives, student needs, special services, resources, facilities, personnel, standards, development, and community relations. Instruction centers on delivery methods, learning styles, planning, evaluation, learning achievement, student engagement, performance evaluation, and student needs. As noted by Sergiovanni and Starratt (1983), even in those instances when supervision and curricular development are separate offices in the school district, the supervisor can act as one of the main sources of feedback to the curriculum developers. At the local school level, the assistant school superintendent or school principal commonly serves both functions.
7. Question 7 is false. Although educational philosophies concerning the school's curriculum do differ, program improvement and student achievement practices are important in every situation. There are a number of strategies to implement in an attempt to align teaching activities and course standards and learning expectations. Curriculum mapping whereby teaching programs and activities are in accord with teaching standards is one strategy that serves to improve curriculum quality. Other strategies to bring teaching into alignment are discussed in other chapters of the book.
8. Question 8 is true. School boards are given the authority for local school curriculum implementation by state legislatures. School boards in turn delegate curriculum responsibilities to the school superintendent and professional staff. District administrators with such titles as coordinator of curriculum work directly with local school principals and teachers to develop, implement, and improve the curricular program for student learning experiences. The knowledge bases for school principals include a number of important administrative competencies including the ability to complete and utilize appropriate research and evaluation, to implement data analysis, to practice staff collaboration, to implement planning and organization, to select primary instructional resources, to determine appropriate student

achievement evaluation procedures, and to implement other strategies for meeting stated curricular goals and objectives.

As noted by Norton (2015), "Adapting instruction and content to a student's success level and learning style has been demonstrated in numerous studies to improve performance" (p. 6). Adjusting student achievement standards to the student's interests and strengths is a strong characteristic of engaged student learning.

9. Question 9 is false. This was answered in Question 5. The creative abilities of teachers are welcomed in the classroom. However, teaching only the subject matter that a teacher wants to teach violates the concept of a school system. Of course, no teachers "teach" only what they want to teach. Or do they? School principals have reported numerous cases when teachers were teaching "outside" the school's prescribed curriculum. In one case, for example, the teacher was showing World War II films at least twice a week in his science class. In another instance, the eighth-grade teacher of "living science" was teaching the material scheduled to be implemented in the eleventh-grade biology course. Apparently, the teacher was teaching but students were not learning; final achievement scores were unsatisfactory.

    The major violations of curriculum commitment come reportedly within the physical fitness and health programs at the high school level. Without attempting to demean the many highly effective physical education (PE) programs visited, too many such programs completely overlooked the health aspects of the curriculum. In addition, when athletic coaches served as PE teachers, the emphasis tended to be placed on developing athletes for boys' sports programs; girls were commonly confined to the volleyball court.

10. Question 10 is true. As previously stated in this chapter, definitions of the term *curriculum* do differ, but most commonly each definition included the important factors of the school activities/experiences provided by the school for the purpose of student learning. In the following chapters, we continue to emphasize the vital importance of curriculum being largely a local function.

KEY IDEAS AND RECOMMENDATIONS

- The U.S. Constitution gives the responsibility of education to the states and to the people. Over time, however, such local control has been reduced by federal mandates that have resulted in top-down curricular controls that inhibit leadership creativity on the part of the school principal in the areas of supervision and curriculum development.

- The chapter supports the recent congressional legislation of Every Student Succeeds. This legislation, if it ultimately becomes law, will serve to give more authority to the states and local school boards in matters of curricular programming. The future will tell if the federal government actually does limit its current controls on education and returns this authority to the various states and its people.
- The emphasis on supervision has changed historically. In the early 1920s, Frederick Taylor's scientific management concepts influenced educational practices as well as the practices in business and industry. This strictly controlled process of supervision ultimately changed to a more democratic process supported by Mary Parker Follett and other authorities of the time. Such later events as Sputnik brought the federal government's interest to the forefront educationally; the need for academic improvement in such curricular fields as mathematics and science was mandated.
- Federal intervention continued thereafter through such programs as the No Child Left Behind legislation. As previously stated, the newest congressional actions related to Every Student Succeeds is accompanied by new skills and knowledge on the part of local school leaders. The foundational concepts of supervision are additionally discussed in chapter 2 and other chapters of this book.
- Not only must future school principals be prepared to assume leadership as effective educational supervisors, but practicing school principals report that they are not sufficiently prepared to assume changes in curriculum planning and development. Preparation programs and in-service development activities must be improved to meet the new challenges. Just doing what other administrative colleagues are doing most likely will not suffice. New knowledge and skills will be needed to meet required changes.
- It was beyond the scope of this chapter to discuss all of the necessary changes needed at the local school to assume the leadership role for curriculum development. New roles for the assistant school principal, for example, are imminent. We recommend the reading of the following resources for considering changes in the administrative roles of both the assistant principal and principal: *The Assistant Principal's Guide: New Strategies for New Responsibilities* (2015), *The Principal as a Learning Leader* (2013), and *The Changing Landscape of School Leadership* (2015).
- Effective administration for the processes of supervision and curriculum is enhanced by a knowledge of research findings and foundational concepts related to human motivation, leadership styles, personnel coordination, student learning styles, and other aspects of effective administration. Chapter 2 opens the discussion of these foundational concepts in detail.
- Supervision is influenced by social and economic conditions of the times in which it is formed. Chapter 1 has discussed the ever-changing views of

education's purposes. The tasks of the school supervisor are to be viewed as dealing with the symptoms of change.

Discussion

1. Give thought to the chapter content related to the pros and cons of federal "involvement" in education. Assume that you, as school principal, were asked the question of local control compared with federal mandates regarding curricular offerings in your school. What is your response to the question?
2. Consider your preparedness as a school principal or as a school principal with whom you are most familiar in regard to the knowledge and skills needed in planning and organizing the school's curriculum. Rate your preparation for such administrative responsibilities. How well were you prepared for such leadership?
3. Assume that you are at the school's Parent Teacher Association's monthly meeting and one parent asks, "Just what do you mean by the school's *curriculum*?" What is your response?
4. Consider the statement that each teacher is a curriculum director when it comes to his or her own classroom. To what extent is the statement true or false?
5. Evaluate the statement, "Supervision is what school personnel do with adults for the purpose of maintaining and changing the operations of the school to influence the attainment of instructional goals and objectives." Name several things that school personnel do administratively to achieve such a purpose.
6. At one of your school's curricular planning meetings a teacher comments, "The theoretical concepts of Taylor, Parker, McGregor, Mayo, and others were set forth years ago and have little reference for what we do today." Give thought to how you would respond.

CASE STUDY

Case 1.1: Changing the Curriculum at Wymore Middle School

George Nelson was in his first year as principal of Wymore Middle School. He was recommended by the search committee and hired primarily because of his experience in curriculum as an assistant principal in another state. His interest in reading led him to believe that every teacher should also be a teacher of reading. That is, a math teacher should teach the vocabulary specifically related to mathematics and develop reading skills through using math story problems. An industrial arts teacher was to place an emphasis on reading as related to directions for building a structure or making a needed repair. Every teacher, according to Principal Nelson, was to give "necessary time" to reading in his or her instructional lesson. This requirement in his opinion would lead to improved reading scores for the school on the state's testing battery. Nelson's plan was to go into effect right after the first six weeks of the school year. Faculty meetings before the six-week deadline gave priority attention to the matter of "Every teacher a teacher of reading." As part of the plan, a pre-test on reading was administered at the beginning of the first six weeks of school. A post-test would reveal the reading improvement that was expected under the program plan.

After the first six weeks, the post-test in reading indeed was administered. The results of the post-test were quite disappointing; no improvement in reading achievement was realized. In a meeting of the school faculty, a teacher of science moved that the reading program that Nelson had implemented be dropped.

"Give the program time," responded Nelson. "All we need is to gain your commitment and double our efforts on what we decided and move ahead for positive results."

During the next six weeks, the program remained in place and faculty meetings continued to focus on each teacher as a teacher of reading. In addition, Nelson increased his classroom visitation schedule for purposes of "needed supervision."

Following the second six weeks of the program, a second reading test was administered to all students. Reading scores in two of the three middle school grades slightly decreased. Nevertheless, Nelson insisted that his reading program continue to the second semester. To help matters, Principal Nelson set up an in-service program for all teachers after school. The program brought various reading specialists to the school for instruction on the topic. The program indeed did continue for the remainder of the school year, but reading scores on additional tests were disappointing.

Nelson drafted a memo to all teachers as follows:

> The school's reading program results have been disappointing. Nevertheless, I will study the results and make a decision before the beginning of the next school year relative to continuing the reading program as planned and implemented. Have a great summer.

Discussion

1. In view of the somewhat limited information set forth in case study 1.1, in one sentence, set forth your thoughts as to why the reading program at Wymore Middle School was unsuccessful.

2. What might you have done initially as a new school principal to initiate an evaluation and assessment program for needed curricular improvement?
3. Give consideration to your preparation as a teacher or school principal. What was the level of instruction that you experienced relative to the administrative process of supervision and curriculum development?
4. Assume that your state legislators passed a bill giving considerable control to school districts and local schools for planning and implementing school curriculum. How prepared do you think that you are personally to assume such responsibilities? Keep in mind that you no longer are just implementing the core curriculum mandated by some other authority. How might you initiate your responsibilities as school principal? What steps might you have to take to prepare yourself for this new role?

REFERENCES

Abbott, S. (2014, August 26). *Hidden curriculum.* The glossary of education reform. Retrieved from http://edglossaryorg/hidden-curriculum.

Berlak, H. (2003, October 3). *From local control to government and corporate takeover of school curriculum: The* No Child Left Behind Act *and the* "Reading First" *Program.* Retrieved from http://wwwleducationandemocracy.org/Resources/Berlak/control.htm

Berliner, D. C., & Biddle, B. J. (1995). *The manufactured crisis: Myths, fraud, and the attack on America's public schools.* Reading, MA: Addison-Wesley.

Donahue v. Copiague USFD, N.Y. 2nd 440, NY Court of Appeals (1979)-Ed. Malpractice.

Finch, C. R., & Crunkilton, J. R. (2015, December 12). *Curriculum development: An overview.* Retrieved from http://oak.ucc.edu/mr/cate592/Mobile_/Curriculum_Development

Follett, M. P. (1924). *Creative experience.* New York, NY: Longmans.

Haddermann, M. I. (1988). State vs. local control of schools. *ERIC Clearinghouse Digest Series Number 24.* Eugene, OR: Eric Clearinghouse on Educational Management.

Lewin, K., Lippitt, R., & White R. (1939). Patterns of aggressive behavior in experimentally created "social climates." *Journal of Social Psychology, 10,* 271–299.

Marsh, C. J., & Willis, G. (2003). *Curriculum: Alternative approaches, ongoing issues.* Upper Saddle River, NJ: Merrill/Prentice Hall.

McNeil, J. D. (2003). *Curriculum: The teacher's initiative* (3rd ed.). Upper Saddle River, NJ: Merrill/Prentice Hall.

Norton, M. S. (2015). *Teachers with the magic: Great teachers change students' lives.* Lanham, MD: Rowman & Littlefield.

Owens, R. G. (2001). *Organizational behavior in education: Instructional leadership and school reform.* Boston, MA: Allyn & Bacon.

Sergiovanni, T. J., & Starratt, R. J. (1983). *Supervision: Human perspectives.* New York, NY: McGraw-Hill.

Spears, H. (1951). *The teacher and curriculum planning.* Upper Saddle River, NJ: Prentice-Hall.

Taylor, F. W. (1911). *Scientific management.* New York, NY: Harper & Row.

Theobald, B., & Troyan, M. (2015, December 10). Congress votes to appeal No Child Left Behind law. *Arizona Republic,* p. 1A.

Webb, L. D., Greer, J. T., Montello, P. A., & Norton, M. S. (1987). *Personnel administration in education: New issues & new needs in human resources management.* Columbus, OH: Merrill.
Wiles, J., & Bondi, J. (1996). *Supervision: A guide to practice.* Englewood Cliffs, NJ: Merrill.

Chapter 2

Foundations of Supervision and Curriculum Development in America

Primary chapter goal: To gain a knowledge of the historical research findings and empirical evidence relating to human motivation, leadership effectiveness, human relations, and supervisory practices that have served as the foundation for effective contemporary practices in education.

CURRICULUM AND SUPERVISION RECOMMENDATIONS FOR 2016 AND THE FUTURE

We will be considering the planning, implementation, and assessment of best practices for supervision and curriculum development in America throughout the chapters of this book. But an important question relative to the matter of best practices is "How did we get there?" That is, what are the foundations of our contemporary thoughts relative to practices that will give educational programs for students the best opportunities to achieve academically? For example, we give considerable thought today to the importance of school climate. What are the factors that brought this about? We talk a great deal about human motivation and coordination as being important for effective supervision and curriculum development. Is it just empirical evidence that brought us to the point of viewing these supervisory practices as important? What activities actually served to influence our best contemporary practices? This chapter opens the discussion on the answers to such questions.

WHAT DOES THE SCIENTIFIC MANAGEMENT ERA HAVE TO OFFER?

Why should school leaders be knowledgeable of supervisory concepts that were prominent more than one hundred years ago? The reason is that such concepts have served as the foundation for many of the administrative "best practices" of our times. The early scientific management era featured the management concepts of Frederick Taylor (1911) and his revolutionary *task system*. Efficiency was the guiding word for the task system that featured four primary components. Managers were to take sole responsibility for determining the completion of each task. If the specific procedures and conditions were followed to the letter, efficiency would be realized and productivity would be assured. The more that the worker carried out controlled procedures to the letter, the better would be the efficiency of the work. The purposes, conditions, equipment, and procedures were not only specified for each task but enforced as well.

Rewards for work outcomes came in proportion to the ability of the worker to follow task procedures and produce efficiently. Failure to do so was also taken into consideration in Taylor's "merit pay" system. Management was to plan the work by dividing tasks and controlling job outcomes. Supervisors hired workers and carried out initial training as to just how the task was to be completed. The concept of division of labor was clear; managers were to plan and control the work and the worker was to do the job according to the specifications set forth. Top-down management was in force nearly one hundred years ago.

Scientific management not only dominated practices at the industrial level, but became important in educational administration as well. The term *efficiency* became a prominent word for educational practices. The question is why? The answer is because it was highly effective; production was positively influenced by the concept. It is reported that educational conferences during this era had sessions on such topics as "How to teach music scientifically" and "Using scientific management to teach the curriculum." Other personnel administration practices such as worker selection, training of personnel, and compensation have been accredited to Taylor's influences as well. Such terms as *educational engineering, task setting, incentive pay, administrative management, division of labor, progress charts, productivity, job structuring, personnel practices,* and *supervisory tasks* were part of the educator's vocabulary during this time period.

Perhaps James L. McConaughy (1918), who was associated with Dartmouth University, summarized education's acceptance of the scientific management concept best. He stated that "this is an age of efficiency. In the eyes of the public no indictment of a school can be more severe than to say it is inefficient" (pp. 191–192). Today's word is *underperforming*. Other educators saw schools as factories in which children, the raw products, were to be shaped and fashioned into products to handle the needs of society. Efficiency permeated the practices of school leaders during this time period just like accountability and student achievement dominate the vocabulary of educators today.

Many other individuals contributed directly to the scientific management concepts. Persons such as Henri Fayol, Henry Gantt, Frank and Lillian Gilbreth, Luther Gulick, Lyndall Urwick, and Max Weber set forth practices that extended scientific management's perspectives and left imprints for contemporary practices. For example, Fayol's fourteen principles of management were published in 1887 in the publication, *Administration Industrielle et Generale*. Among Fayol's fourteen principles were terms that remain in our supervisory vocabulary today. A few examples are as follows:

> Chain of Command—Fayol used the term *scalar chain* to describe the chain of superiors ranging from the ultimate authority to the lowest ranks. He insisted that the lines of authority should be clear and followed at all times.
>
> Esprit de Corps—Managers should foster and maintain teamwork, team spirit, and a sense of unity and togetherness among employees. Today we view these concepts in terms of *morale, collaboration, climate,* and *cooperation*.
>
> Order or Coordination—Human and material resources should be coordinated to be in the right place at the right time.
>
> Initiative—Employees should be encouraged to develop and carry out plans for improvement.
>
> Division of Work—The object of division of work is improved efficiency through reduction of waste, increased output, and a simplification of job training.
>
> Unity of Direction or Purpose—Similar activities that are directed toward a singular goal should be grouped together under one manager. Mission, vision, and purpose are foremost in today's thoughts of program improvement.

The "controlling nature" of Common Core State Standards (CCSS) is revealed in one instance by its statements regarding the selection of instructional resources. For example, when new instructional materials are needed, CCSS sets forth the following measures: (1) What percentage of school expenditures on new instructional materials (purchases or developed) is spent on resource aligned with CCSS? (2) What percentage of existing materials has school instructional staff reviewed to determine their alignment with the CCSS—and revised if necessary? And (3) What percentage of teacher-created lessons and units addresses agreed-upon (CCSS) criteria? Goals are established by the CCSS and all other instructional activities must align with them (The Aspen Institute, 2013).

Fayol's principles later were amplified by such people as Chester Barnard and Henry L. Gantt, whose work will be discussed later. In any case, Fayol's components and processes of an organization most likely will be reviewed necessarily today by any person seeking administrative design information. Fayol's major contribution to supervision perhaps was his efforts in helping to answer the question: What is management? His five functions of management have tended to stand the test of time; the functions set forth were revolutionary. His acronym of POCCC was revolutionary at the time:

PLANNING—to examine the future and develop a plan of action
ORGANIZING—to build human and material resources and build up lines of authority
COMMANDING—to instill a sense of mission; maintain personnel activity
COORDINATING—to bind in all together, unify, and harmonize the effort
CONTROLLING—to monitor and adjust

Which of these terms would not be familiar to educational supervisors today? Although we might want to change the names of commanding and controlling to visioning and assessing/adjusting, the purposes of the terms are compatible. As stated by Norton, Kelly, and Battle (2012), "The first basic ingredient of leadership is guiding vision. The leader has a clear idea of what he wants to do" (p. 38).

Other "contemporary terms" that evolved from the scientific management era included *specialization, on-the-job-training, job analysis, span of control, line/staff positions, chief executive officer, job description, bureaucracy, rationality, professional management, principles of standards, division of work, prescribed competence, specifications, incentive pay, inefficiency, accountability,* and *principle of definition.* The scientific management era, despite its top-down view of supervision, gave contemporary supervision many of its foundational concepts.

Fayol (1916) underscored the concepts of scientific management in his statement that "the organization is a complex of mechanisms, rules, laws, and principles. In essence the organization is a machine, the administrator is the operator" (p. 23).

Urwick and Gulick (1937) extended the work of Fayol by establishing the well-known and utilized paradigm POSDCoRB that set forth the seven major tasks of all managers. Planning, Organization, Staffing, Directing, Coordinating, Reporting, and Budgeting gave new directions for leaders in business and industry but was accepted by professional educators as well. For the most part, the paradigm is practiced by school leaders in our contemporary schools.

HOW FRANK AND LILLIAN GILBRETH INCREASED WORK PRODUCTIVITY BY 200 PERCENT

It is possible that you might recall the movie *Cheaper by the Dozen*, based to some extent on the lives of Frank and Lillian Gilbreth. The Gilbreths were industrial engineers who focused on efficiency by using such methods as time and motion studies. Job simplification was their main concern. How can a bricklayer lay bricks more efficiently? By studying the movements of bricklayers and designing their equipment and positioning of bricks so that physical movements were best, reportedly the worker's productivity increased by an estimated 200 percent (Griffin, 1987).

GANTT'S IDEAS ON SCIENTIFIC MANAGEMENT ARE RELEVANT TODAY

Henry Gantt devised charts for record keeping, time and motion, cost accounting, planning and controlling, task setting, and other business and industrial practices that remain in practice today. In 1887 Gantt worked directly with Frederick Taylor in applying scientific management principles to the work of the Midvale Steel and Bethlehem Steel companies.

Gantt charts (1961) were employed on major infrastructure projects including the Hoover Dam and interstate highway system and continue to be an important tool in project and program management. He expressed the view that the ideal industrial company would be identified as one in which every worker had a specific daily task and in turn would receive a proper reward for quality production. One of Gantt's highly referenced publications is titled *Organizing for Work*, published in 1919 and reprinted in 1973.

We, of course, are not making a plea to return to the mechanistic era demonstrated by scientific management procedures; rather the plea is for school leaders to be knowledgeable of the foundational contributions that many individuals made to present-day administrative knowledge and practice. Historically, concepts of administrative practices come and go. The best practices leave us with better ways and means for improving what we do administratively. The chaff falls through the cracks of the ever flowing changes in administrative practice.

Other individuals such as Max Weber, Elwood Cubberley, and John Bobbitt made significant contributions to the scientific management era. Nevertheless, times changed and a new era of human relations became prominent, led by Mary Parker Follett and others. Follett's recommended changes to supervisory practices were revolutionary.

THE HUMAN RELATIONS MOVEMENT: SCHOOLS ARE PEOPLE

Scientific management was at its peak during the years of 1911–1918. By 1920, however, the concept of workers as machines took a deserved turn toward the concept that organizations are people. The focus of administration centered on the human element of organizations. However, the turn to human cooperation was not initiated by local school educators, but was stressed by such individuals as Tead and Metcalf, who were professors of industrial science and political science, respectively. To the best of our knowledge, the first book ever published on the specific topic of personnel administration was authored by Tead and Metcalf in 1920. As the authors stated in the preface of the book, "The purpose of this book is to set forth the principles and the best prevailing practices in the field of administration of human relations in industry" (p. vii). Additionally, "The new focus in administration is to be the human element. The new center of attention is the individual person, the worker" (p. 1). The need to gain the human cooperation and the goodwill and interest of the workers had become the major problem of production.

The Human Relations Movement Takes Center Stage

Which of the following terms would you consider contemporary terms in education?: *commitment, coordination, democratic leadership, motivators, involvement, integration, basic needs, leadership styles, collaboration, job satisfaction, human relations, Hawthorne effect, communication, cooperation,* and *self-direction*. Each of these terms loomed important in the research, literature, and practices of the human relations era that was initiated near the beginning of the year 1920. This era would prove to have an everlasting influence on organizational supervision in business, industry, and education.

If Taylor could be considered the father of the scientific management movement, Mary Parker Follett could be considered the mother of the human relations era. Follett's book *Creative Experience* (1924) was revolutionary; its focus on social ethics and the human element in organizations led other individuals to seek and report on other factors of organizational life that influenced the behavior of the individual worker. Follett believed that the primary concern of any organization was the building and maintenance of dynamic, yet harmonious human relations. Organizational harmony was fostered primarily by the feature of *coordination*. She placed the worker in the direct line of organizational cooperation. *Direct contact* was a first necessity.

A worker's responsibility for required tasks had to be in the direct line of communication regardless of his or her role in the organization. Both vertical and horizontal communication were necessary for cooperative relationships to be effective.

In addition, according to Follett's concepts, employees had to be involved in work decisions at the outset of decision making. Being informed only after a decision was made would not lead to the needed conditions of employee motivation and positive morale. All factors surrounding a work situation had to be related to one another if coordination was to result. The factors of participative involvement, ongoing relationships, internal communication, and social ethics must be implemented on a continuing basis if cooperation was to be realized. When cooperation is in force, individuals are prone to accept personal responsibility for work outcomes (Follett, 1940).

The *integration* concepts of Follett were revolutionary. She argued that conflicts within the organization are resolved best through the process of integration whereby the talents of each individual are elicited and discussed. Such discussion would lead both parties to a solution that served the best interests of all those concerned. Authoritarian measures were unproductive in attempts to resolve conflicts; compromise was much more effective for conflict problem solutions.

Follett influenced other individuals such as Elton Mayo, Fritz Roethlisberger, William Dickson, Kurt Lewin, and colleagues who made major contributions to the human relations movement. Such matters as working conditions, informal group influences, employee behavior, and leadership styles were among the topics given primary attention by these research authorities. It remains important for school principals and other school leaders to be knowledgeable of the research work of these scholars.

Mayo came to the United States from Australia in the early 1920s. As an industrial psychologist, he was interested in such problems as worker turnover and employee motivation. While a member of Harvard University, he and his colleagues studied the work atmosphere at a Philadelphia textile plant. The working climate at the plant was found to have high levels of monotonous work; the results were worker boredom and low production. By inserting such "innovations" as break periods and other incentives, turnover was virtually eliminated at the work site. At the time, Mayo and his colleagues were convinced that the external benefits were the factors that led to improved job satisfaction and higher production.

In follow-up studies at the Hawthorne plant near Chicago, Illinois, Mayo and others inserted other changes within the work site. For example, when the lighting in the plant was increased, production was increased. But when the lighting in the plant was reduced, production increased once more. It was concluded that the physical conditions in the plant were not responsible for production increases; rather it was the attention given to the workers themselves that brought about the production increases. This phenomenon became known as the *Hawthorne effect*.

THE INFLUENCE OF INFORMAL GROUPS IN THE ORGANIZATION

The early research of Fritz Roethlisberger and William Dickson (1939) opened the door for new thoughts about the influence of informal groups on organizational practices and production outcomes. These researchers authored the book *Management and the Worker*. In experiments in a telephone company, termed the *Bank Wiring Experiments*, the researchers observed the social relationships and behaviors of the workers. The informal group members were found to be able to control the production output of their coworkers in regard to too much output or too little output. Social pressure accompanied by group sanctions tended to control production levels more so than orders from the formal plant managers. The fact that informal groups were active in all organizations resulted in giving renewed attention to their involvement in workplace decisions. New employees tend to learn "how it's done around here" early in their employment.

WHAT ABOUT ADMINISTRATIVE LEADERSHIP?

This section opens with a brief quiz on leadership and related personnel practices. Give your answer to each question and then check the correct response at the end of the quiz.

Pre-Quiz

1. School leaders must be knowledgeable of group processes because
    a. workers respond to management as individuals rather than as groups.
    b. specialization creates the most efficient organization of a work group.
    c. workers respond to management as members of an organization, not as individuals.
    d. the presence of informal groups is seldom found in effective organizations.

2. Which statement was found to be true in a research study of leadership styles?

a. Laissez-faire leadership (free-reign approach) resulted in a higher level of work production.
b. Democratic leadership resulted in inferior work quality and self-direction.
c. Authoritarian leadership resulted in higher levels of work productivity but lower levels of cooperation, morale, and self-direction.
d. Authoritarian leadership actually resulted in higher levels of worker cooperation.

3. Research work by Mayo and others made it clear that

   a. the physical makeup of the organization is less important for worker productivity than the factors that relate to the attention given to the human element.
   b. the physical makeup of an organization is of primary importance for fostering worker motivation and commitment to the organization's purposes.
   c. human relations within the organization might be important for individual friendships but are of little importance as related to personnel retention and commitment to the organization's objectives.
   d. the time spent on attempting to "make workers happy" would be much better spent in implementing such practices as time and motion studies or setting stricter rules on matters of "soldiering" (workers giving the impression that they were working hard but really not doing so).

4. The term that might be best to explain the human relations era is:

   a. democratic supervision
   b. positive working relationships
   c. integration for conflict resolution
   d. organizations are people
   e. all of the above

5. Which term would be most appropriate to explain the features of the human relations era?

   a. controlled conditions for production
   b. mechanistic work production
   c. democratic supervision
   d. science (behavioral) of administration

e. social system

Quiz Answers

The answers are 1. c; 2. c; 3. a; 4. a; 5. c.

Further explanations of these responses are provided in the following section. We must keep in mind that a scientific theory serves to support a hypothesis or group of hypotheses that have been supported by repeated research and testing. A tested theory gives us a best concept or means for implementing a practice or making a decision about what steps are most appropriate or implementing certain procedures. Further research or additional empirical experience might lead to additional confidence in the theory or perhaps cause us to reconsider the contentions.

The human relations era that arose in the second decade of the twentieth century gave rise to the development of personnel services in business, industrial, and educational organizations. As noted previously, in 1920 Tead and Metcalf spoke early about the importance of personnel services in organizations, but it wasn't until 1935 that the organization of personnel administrators evolved and by 1951 the group became the American Association of Examiners; ultimately the group endorsed the contemporary title of American Association of School Personnel Administrators (Gibson & Hunt, 1965). In 1938, Chester Barnard authored *The Functions of the Executive*, a book that many authorities consider to be one of the most important books ever written in the field of educational administration. His concepts dominated the focus of organizational administration from 1938 and forward. Today, Barnard's work continues to influence contemporary administrative and supervisory practices; his contributions are discussed in the next section of the book.

THE BEHAVIORAL SCIENCE MOVEMENT AND SUPERVISORY CONCEPTS

In one sense, the behavioral science movement brought together the scientific management era and the human resources era. That is, the concept considered organizations as possessing a structural element and a human element. These two elements are always operating to influence human behavior and the achievement of work activities. In brief, behavior is a function of role and personality: $B = f(R \times P)$. What is generally viewed as social behavior is based on the expectation of the worker's role being carried out and the worker's need dispositions result in the worker's observed behavior (Getzels & Guba, 1957).

Today's school principal would be quite familiar with the terms *effective communication, commitment of employees for effective performance*, and *formulation of organizational purposes and objectives*. These three principle tasks, according to Barnard, are required of each "executive" if organizational effectiveness is to be realized. In the words of Barnard (1938),

> An organization comes into being when (1) there are persons able to communicate with each other (2) who are willing to contribute to action (3) to accomplish a common purpose. The elements of an organization therefore (1) communication; (2) willingness to serve; and (3) common purpose. . . . For the continued existence of an organization either *effectiveness* or *efficiency* is necessary; and the longer the life, the more necessary both are. (p. 82)

Barnard's concepts loom important in the rest of this book. As can be clearly understood, it is not always new revolutionary concepts that determine positive program improvement; rather a thorough knowledge and skill needed to implement those high-quality empirical and basic research findings serve us well as we move to improve curriculum and supervision practices in our schools.

Barnard's thoughts about efficiency and effectiveness set the stage for many research studies on human behavior and effective program practices. Such concepts hold important implications for school leaders in their efforts to implement highly effective supervision practices in their schools.

IS JOB SATISFACTION REALLY IMPORTANT?

During the scientific management era, it was believed that just the incentive rewards resulting from a worker's high production was enough to bring about job satisfaction. However, during the behavioral science era thoughts about job satisfaction were altered by studies by such people as Frederick Herzberg and associates, Douglas McGregor, Victor Vroom, and others. Their studies resulted in new thinking about the importance of job satisfaction and the factors that influenced it on the job.

Motivation refers to a process governing individual choices among different forms of voluntary activities. It is a complex of forces, drives, needs, tensions, statuses, or other mechanisms that start and maintain voluntary activity directed toward the achievement of personal goals. Two classifications of theory are content or substantive theories and process theories. Content theories attempt to specify only what motivates behavior: needs theory; existence, relatedness, growth (ERG) theory; and two-factor theory. For example, one might use Maslow's needs theory (1987) to motivate employees.

Maslow's theory, which suggests that humans are motivated by a hierarchy of needs progressing through the psychological, social, and psychological needs, has powerful implications for school leaders. It suggests that bureaucratic organizations, which seek to motivate employees through money or merely providing a secure job, confine human development to the lower levels of the need hierarchy. The implications for managers were that jobs and interpersonal relations could be redesigned to create conditions for personal growth that would simultaneously help organizations meet their goals and objectives.

Maslow's hierarchy of needs (1987) that serve as motivators for action are as follows:

1. Psychological Needs—Needs necessary to sustain life.
2. Safety Needs—Avoiding physical danger; providing security.
3. Belongingness and Love Needs—Feeling of being wanted and accepted.
4. Esteem Needs—Self-respect, achievement, and esteem given by others.
5. Self-Actualization Needs—Become the person one can become.

According to the theory, a need is a potential motivator until it is realized or satisfied. As the need is satisfied, it becomes ineffective as a motivator and the next higher-order need becomes the motivator for the individual. Self-actualization is the need to grow and develop psychologically, to find one's identity and realize one's potential. It is a need that is never completely satisfied. Often included is the job itself; opportunity to perform interesting, challenging, and meaningful work.

The competence motive is expressed by teachers as a desire for job mastery. Teachers so motivated work to apply their skills, abilities, and competencies against the challenges of the work. Each success reinforces their image of being personally worthy. Is this contention possibly the faults underlying controlled methods such as those set forth by core curricula? Our interviews with professional staff personnel have revealed two important results. First, great teachers are first to "demand" opportunities for personal growth and development. Secondly, if effective supervision procedures are not implemented in the teacher's growth plan, they are likely to find another position where such growth is available.

The idea of integrating the needs of individuals and organizations became a powerful force for supervisory improvement. Herzberg, McGregor, Guba and Getzels, and others began to show how bureaucratic structures, leadership styles, and work organization could be modified to create "enriched" motivating jobs that would encourage people to exercise their capacities for self-control and creativity. As a result, alternatives to bureaucratic organization began to emerge. Particular attention was focused on the idea of making employees feel more useful and important by giving them meaningful work, more autonomy, greater responsibility, and due recognition. Job enrichment was combined with more democratic and participative employee-centered styles of leadership. Maslow's hierarchy suggested a whole new continuum of means through which employees could be motivated at all levels of the need hierarchy and without necessarily having to pay for it financially.

ADMINISTRATOR AND TEACHER NEED DEFICIENCIES

Motivation theories commonly are classified under two major headings: content theories, and process theories. Content theories are exemplified by human need theories. For example, Maslow's needs hierarchy contends that certain lower-level needs must be met before other needs will serve as motivators for the individual. Process theories focus more on what factors are most influential in motivating human beings. That is, how are people motivated and how the motivation process occurs. For example, Vroom's expectancy theory states that a person is motivated if the three factors of existence, relatedness, and instrumentality can be satisfied in the person's mind at appropriate levels. Both motivation theories are discussed in the following section.

Maslow did not intend to propose a motivational recipe for administrative use, but rather a thinking framework for analysis for thinking about human motivation. For example, it does not make much sense to motivate at the upper levels of the hierarchy (esteem, self-actualization) if a real teacher's needs center on lower levels of safety and security. Many studies have been completed relative to the needs of teachers. Although teacher needs differ, there are certain commonalities. We completed an analysis of several different studies on this matter and found that self-actualization ranked first among five needs of teachers. The esteem need ranked second, autonomy ranked third, security/safety ranked fourth, and socialization ranked fifth. Because these studies were conducted before the 9/11 terrorist act, perhaps these rankings might have changed to some extent. Security and safety, for example, might be a higher need for teachers today. In view of the top-down controls that have come with such federal programs as the core curriculum, autonomy also would be expected to move up the hierarchy ladder. Maslow's theory has been studied, praised, altered, and criticized over the years. However, the theory has done much to help focus attention on needs and the human dimension of organizations. In lists of basic principles of supervision, one recommendation that most always is included is "know your staff." But just what is it that the supervisor should know about them? For purposes of motivation and engagement, Maslow's hierarchy of human motivations would loom important.

One could argue that Maslow's motivation theory was presented to them in Psych 101. The question is, To what extent has it been implemented in their leadership role as a school principal?

SIGNIFICANT SUPERVISION CONCEPTS OF HUMAN MOTIVATION

If indeed schools are people, their behavior looms important in any discussion of effective supervision. Important research findings on human behavior during the behavioral science and postmodern science eras were completed by Douglas McGregor, Frederick Herzberg, Egon Guba and Jacob Getzels, Rensis Likert, Andrew Halpin, and others. A summary of several of these individuals' contributions is set forth in the following section. In reviewing these concepts, consider just how each is evident in contemporary practice.

McGregor's Concepts of Theory Behavior

Taylor's scientific management views of workers having little intelligence, ambition, or initiative were discussed previously. McGregor's (1960) Theory Y challenged these negative views of the worker and set forth several revolutionary concepts of worker potential in his book, *The Human Side of Enterprise*. McGregor provided new insights into the importance of the worker and further opened the door to effective programs of human resources in all organizations. In addition, Theory Y pointed out the potential of workers and their ability to contribute to the goals of the organization. The involvement of the worker in organizational matters was viewed as essential for achieving the purposes of the organization. McGregor (1960) underscored the importance of providing high expectations for a worker's performance. High expectations would lead to high performance accomplishments. Since that time, we have seen the concept of "high expectations" become highly important in student achievement.

Theory Y sets forth six concepts relating to human potential as follows:

1. The expenditure of physical and mental effort in work is as natural as play or rest.
2. People will exercise self-direction and self-control in the service of objectives to which they are committed.
3. Commitment to objectives is a function of the rewards associated with their achievement.
4. The average human being learns, under proper conditions, not only to accept but to seek responsibility.
5. The capacity to exercise a relatively high degree of imagination, ingenuity, and creativity in the solution of organizational problems is widely, not narrowly, distributed in the population.
6. Under the conditions of modern industrial life, the intellectual potentials of the average human being are only partially utilized (pp. 47–48).

Frederick Herzberg's Two-Factor Theory of Job Satisfaction

Herzberg, Mausner, and Snyderman (1959) established the fact that those factors that bring about job satisfaction, with the possible exception of salary, differ from those that result in job dissatisfaction. For example, the concept postulates that while a certain factor is likely to bring about job satisfaction, its absence does not in turn result in job dissatisfaction. Factors such as achievement, recognition, work itself, responsibility, advancement, and salary, when present, tend to result in increased job satisfaction. However, when these factors are not present, this would not bring about dissatisfaction. Factors such as company policy, supervision practices, interpersonal relations with supervisory personnel, and working conditions are those that lead to job dissatisfaction.

Interestingly enough, studies over the years related to school personnel support Herzberg's findings. For teachers, principals, and others the motivational factors of achievement, recognition, work itself, responsibility, and interpersonal relationships with students have been identified as most important for job satisfaction. The question to be addressed is, "How are these factors implemented in effective supervisory practices?"

Getzels and Guba Social Systems Theory

Getzels and Guba's (1957) theory gave impetus to the study of school systems as human organizations that were always interacting between the structural or nomothetic dimension and the human or idiographic dimension of an organization. Many authorities consider this concept as one of the most important ever submitted for directing the behavior of school leaders. It is beyond the scope of the chapter to discuss the concept in full detail. However, the crux of the social system concept is set forth in the "formula" $B = f(R \times P)$; the behavior outcome (B) within the social system is determined by the institutional or nomothetic role and the individual's personality (P). The role represents positions, status with the institution, which is defined by the purposes and nature of the organization. The individual's personality and need disposition constitute the human or idiographic dimension of the organization. These two dimensions are always interacting to determine the behaviors of individual workers.

Halpin and Croft (1962) point out that only one of these dimensions might keep the organization "afloat" if working effectively, but only for a brief period of time. Both dimensions must be operating effectively if the organization is going to be effective over time. That is, the school principal must give full attention to the structural and human dimensions of the school to reach successfully the school program's goals and objectives

VROOM'S EXPECTANCY THEORY OF MOTIVATION

Motivation theory attempts to explain how and why individuals are able to achieve their goals. *Expectancy theory* is an attempt to predict motivation outcomes of non-verbal communication. Vroom's expectancy theory (1964) supports the belief that workers put forth the required effort and are more productive when they perceive a relationship among effort, performance, and reward. Motivation, in this concept, depends on the degree to which the outcome is desirable or undesirable (*valence*), the belief that an action will lead to the desired reward (*instrumentality*), and the degree of certainty that a given act will yield the desired results (*expectancy*). Figure 2.1 illustrates the theory.

STOP FOR A MOMENT AND THINK ABOUT ONE DILEMMA

A theory remains as just a good idea until it is actually seriously considered and implemented in practice. If by some scientific miracle a cure was found to the growing problem of dementia and Alzheimer's disease, physicians around the world would waste no time in implementing it in their practices. Yet, in education, numerous positive research findings for education have been found and recommended but set aside as education moves on with the same "ineffective" practices. Student retention, teacher load, student learning styles, and human motivation results are such study examples.

WORK OUTCOME

EXPECTANCY >>>>	Can I Achieve the Work Outcome? >>>>	No—Results in no motivation
	Yes	
INSTRUMENTALITY >>>>	Does Work Outcome Lead to Reward? >>>>	No—Results in no motivation
	Yes	
VALENCE >>>>	Is Work Something I Value? >>>>	No—Results in no motivation
	Yes	

WORK MOTIVATION

Figure 2.1 Vroom's Motivational Theory

We submit that both empirical and basic research evidence must become a required focus of school activities and practices in supervision and curriculum development. If the purposes of this book's message are to be achieved, school principals must become consumers, dispensers, and users of quality educational research.

SUPERVISION AT THE SCHOOL DISTRICT LEVEL

The focus of supervision in this book is primarily on the school principal or supervision that is provided by an assistant principal or individual within the local school. We do realize that people working at the school district level commonly perform important supervision and curriculum services that affect the local school as well. A study of 211 supervisors at the school district level was administered with the following results. Of the 211 participating supervisors, 62 of them had different position titles. Although it is not the purpose here to report all of the supervisory titles held, at least two people in the study held the following titles in their position:

Instructional Specialist (the most common title)
Assistant Superintendent
Assistant Superintendent for Instruction
Instructional Services Administrator
Director, Curriculum and Instruction
Special Programs Coordinator
Coordinator of Curriculum and Supervision
Director of Special Programs
Coordinator of Secondary School Curriculum and Instruction

Fifteen specific functions were listed and respondents were provided the opportunity to write in other responsibilities. The results of these supervisors' main position responsibilities are listed in table 2.1.

Numerous other responsibilities were listed by the participating supervisors. Budget development, computer services/technical services, diagnostic testing, materials dissemination, mediating conflict (relative to curricular matters), textbook/e-book selection, and other responsibilities were mentioned by some supervisors. Most supervisors at the school district level conceived of their job as a "coordinator" or "facilitator." In addition, most supervisors viewed their role as a service role as opposed to a control position. The exception to this view was held primarily by participants in the position of assistant school superintendent or in some cases as director.

Ninety-seven of the 211 district supervisors reported a twelve-month contract while eleven-, ten-, and nine-month contracts were held by 24, 43, and 26 supervisors, respectively. It should be noted that the study partici-

Table 2.1

Function	Number of Responses
Staff Development	150
Curriculum Development	144
Classroom Visitation/Observation	140
Program Evaluation/Standards	138
Teaching Strategies/Methods	129
Articulation of Curriculum	114
Instructional Materials Selection	105
Community/Parent Relations	97
Research Development (Curriculum)	91
Curriculum Policy/Regulation Development	83
Pupil Achievement Evaluation	80
Organizational Climate Development	78
Teacher Evaluation	72
Master Teacher (Modeling Activities)	62

pants served in schools with widely different school student populations. School district student enrollments differed from less than 1,000 students to more than 45,000 students. Of course, some were elementary school districts, some were secondary school districts with both middle and high school enrollments, and some were high school districts only.

Position Description for a Local School Instructional Supervisor

A position description for a local instructor supervisor is illustrated here. Position descriptions for an instructional supervisor differ in relation to the specific duties, size of the school, and the supervisory support assumed by the central district office of the school district. It is common for the local school instructional supervisor to be responsible for curriculum development as well.

Position Description for a Local School Instructional Supervisor
Position Description
Instructional Supervisor
Wymore High School

1. Position Qualifications
2.
   - Master's Degree in Secondary Education, Teaching License
   - Minimum of three years of teaching experience in secondary schools
   - Course work and experience in research, curriculum, and instructional methodology
   - Competent in the operation and utilization of instructional technology

3. Supervisor
4. Responsible to the local school assistant school principal or principal as assigned
5. Salary
6. Salary is assigned as set forth in the teachers' salary schedule plus $4,000 for supervisory position and $6,500 for two extra months of service
7. Assigned Duties and Responsibilities
8.
   - Responsible for keeping abreast of current research pertaining to curriculum and supervision
   - Responsible for recommending for planning, implementing, and evaluating the school's curriculum program including the co-curricular educational activities provided within the school
   - Works with committees of teachers, administrators, and school patrons in initiating, evaluating, and assessing the school's curriculum program
   - Supports teacher personnel in developing their individual improvement plan
   - Serves as a mentor or coach for teaching personnel as assigned
   - Serves as a supervisor for establishing achievement standards for courses taught
   - Helps in the development of meaningful report card system that encompasses the concepts of individualized student performance
   - Works with teachers in the development of effective lesson plans for each subject taught
   - Observes teacher performance for formative purposes and not for summative purposes

- Supervises the implementation of effective testing procedures for classroom implementation
- Works with the assistant school principal or principal and other school instructional supervisors
- Designs in-service development programs and workshops including the development of subject/grade curriculum guides
- Gives special attention to orientation programs for teachers new to the school
- Monitors the articulation of the curriculum program
- Models effective teaching methods and strategies for teachers upon request (modeling)
- Takes a leadership role in assessing the results of teacher evaluations
- Cooperates with the assistant principal and principal in the development of positive school climate activities and reports
- Serves as a consumer, dispenser, and user of quality educational research
- Cooperates with teachers in programs for staff development
- Position is viewed as a service role as opposed to a line administrative position

9. Position Perspective

OVERRIDING PRINCIPLES OF CURRICULUM DEVELOPMENT

The procedures of curriculum planning vary from system to system, school to school, and classroom to classroom, but they are logical, consistent, and identifiable in each situation. Other basic principles include the following concepts:

1. The quality in educational programming has priority in America's goals, objectives, values, and beliefs. Education's importance for sustaining a democratic nation, giving each individual a fair and unfettered chance in the race of life, and supporting a free enterprise system, has been addressed historically as essential by presidents and other leaders of the nation.
2. Curriculum itself must be dynamic and is ever changing as new developments and societal needs arise. Meeting the needs and interests of each student ties closely to this concept of change. Just what constitutes the appropriate curriculum, how it is to be disseminated in the classroom, and how to address the individual differences of learners all constitute the work of curriculum directors and supervisors in

America's schools. The guiding role of an effective instructional supervisor rests in his or her ability to connect curriculum with current curriculum implementation.
3. No master curriculum will serve all schools, but education should be viewed as a local function in relation to the guiding legislation of individual states. Education historically has been viewed as a national concern, a state responsibility, and a local function.
4. Many individuals should participate in curriculum planning, but local participation by teachers, administrative leaders, parents, and school community members is of primary importance. Parents and school community members must have a significant role in decision making about what students should learn and what the school must provide for all students.

KEY IDEAS AND RECOMMENDATIONS

- Purpose looms important relative to worker motivation and job satisfaction. Its accomplishment depends on the leader's understanding and ability to establish a commitment to purposes for which the workers themselves have helped to develop. Without purpose, workers' behaviors are lost in a meaningless vacuum.
- Significant concepts of organizational effectiveness have been set forth historically. Such knowledge must be studied and assessed as a means for improving current practice.
- Education has been negligent in the areas of research. Educational professionals should become consumers, dispensers, and implementers of valid and reliable research findings. School principals must be prepared to assume a research posture for effective supervisor and curriculum leadership. Important findings have been revealed in research studies concerning student learning, student retention in grades, learning styles, human motivation, and other important phenomena concerning human behavior. What is needed is the serious consideration of research results and their applications in current practice.
- Principals and teachers must pay attention to theory. Theories concerning student learning are especially important for teachers. The teacher's responsibility really is not showing students what they should learn; rather their accountability is to make certain that each student learns. As noted by Phillips and Soltis (1991), it is the teacher who must make the best sense of what is known about how to foster learning in the classroom.
- Job satisfaction and human motivation have been studied primarily in relation to business and industry. However, related studies in education

have served to identify those factors that tend to result in employee motivation, satisfaction, and retention.
- Attention to individual worker interests and needs is important. However, informal groups within the organization have been found to have considerable influence concerning work production.
- Today's educational "innovations" and supervisory practices commonly are founded on the important work and theories of many scholars historically.
- The basic aim of science is to find general explanations termed *theories*. It is important to remember that a theory represents a valid conclusion that has been generalized on the basis of logical arguments and the testing of hypotheses. If a hypothesis has been found to be valid through testing procedures used and when the hypothesis serves to explain phenomena generally in the science, the term *theory* is applied. John Dewey (1929) stated that theory in the end is the "most practical of all things, because this widening of the range of attention beyond nearby purpose and desire eventually results in the creation of wider and farther-reaching purposes and enables us to use a much wider and deeper range of conditions and means than were expressed in the observation of primitive practical purposes" (p. 17).
- Supervision focuses on helping personnel grow and develop.

Discussion

1. Take a moment to review one of the chapter concepts of employee motivation (Herzberg, Maslow, Vroom, or others). Consider the extent to which it reflects the view of factors that serve as motivation for you.
2. This chapter focused on the contention that many early studies and findings of human motivation and job satisfaction are applicable for use by supervisors in schools today. To what extent do you agree with this contention?
3. Purpose, communication, and commitment were three factors identified by Barnard as essential for an effective organization. Consider the school in which you work or a school that you know best. On a scale of 1 (low) to 5 (high), how would you rank the school in relation to these three factors? Give a brief statement of support for each ranking.
4. Give thought to the scientific management concept discussed in this chapter. To what extent do you believe the basic features of that era are still identifiable in today's school programs?
5. Three specific eras were discussed: scientific management, human relations, and behavioral science eras. Give thought to present-day

administrative practices in education. What name would you give to current practices? List several features that define your chosen title.

CASE STUDY

Case 2.1: Jump Start for a Teacher in Need

Max Barkley was a math teacher at Northeast Middle School. The middle school was being contained at a newly constructed high school until a nearby middle school could be expanded to handle the increased student enrollment. Vera Vanhusen, coordinator of curriculum for the school district, was forming a curriculum committee to revise the math program at the middle school level. She approached Max regarding his participation on the committee because he was the logical representative for Northeast Middle School at this time.

Max was reluctant to serve on the committee. "I served on one of these committees once before and it was strictly a waste of time," said Max. "Quite frankly, I know what I'm teaching and wish to pass on the invitation to waste my time again."

"Well, Max," responded Miss Vanhusen, "you are the logical one to represent your school on this important curriculum project, so I would like to see you there."

Max reluctantly showed up for the first curriculum meeting, but sat back in his chair and said nothing during the first meeting of the committee when purposes and schedules were being discussed.

Max showed up late for the second meeting, indicating that he had to complete a lesson plan for the next day's classes. He attended the third planning meeting of the curriculum committee as well but sat silently for the most part.

The planning committee made notable progress during the first meetings of the committee and were in the process of discussing learning goals and objectives for one course in Algebra 1. The committee was "stumped" for a moment on just what to include in the curriculum guide when Max awakened and said, "Well, I do have one effective method for teaching that particular subject matter" and briefly explained it to the committee members.

"Max," said Miss Vanhusen, "would you write a page or so on that technique? It would be an excellent piece to place in the enrichment section of the guide."

"Do you mean that you want me to write a page on the technique that I just explained for inclusion in the curriculum guide?" asked Max.

"Certainly," responded Vera Vanhusen. Members of the committee shook their heads in agreement.

Max's demeanor changed dramatically. He actually became a committee member. His ideas and work commitment were quite satisfactory. When the curriculum guide was completed and it was time to select a specific textbook for the courses at hand, a six-member committee was asked to serve on the materials selection committee. Who was the first teacher to volunteer for the committee. You are right! Max's hand went up first.

Discussion

1. Quickly review the several motivation theories set forth in this chapter. Which of them might be most appropriate for explaining the change in motivation on the part of Max Barkley? Briefly explain your selection(s).

REFERENCES

The Aspen Institute. (2013, September). *Implementation of the Common Core State Standards: A transition guide for school-level leaders.* Washington, DC: Author.
Barnard, C. I. (1938). *The functions of the executive.* Cambridge, MA: Harvard University Press.
Dewey, J. (1929). *Sources of a science of education.* New York, NY: Liveright.
Fayol, H. (1916). *General and industrial management.* London, UK: Sir Isaac Pitman and Sons. (Original work published 1916)
Follett, M. P. (1924–1940). *Creative experience.* New York, NY: Longmans.
Gantt, H. L. (1961). *Gantt on management.* New York, NY: American Management Association and the American Society of Mechanical Engineers.
Getzels, J. W., & Guba, E. G. (1957). Social behavior and the administrative process. *School Review, 65*(4), 423–441.
Gibson, R. O., & Hunt, H. C. (1965). *The school personnel administrator.* Boston, MA: Houghton-Mifflin.
Griffin, R. W. (1987). *Management.* Boston, MA: Houghton-Mifflin.
Halpin, A. W., & Croft, D. B. (1962). *The organizational climate of schools.* Washington, DC: U.S. Office of Education.
Herzberg, F., Mausner, B., & Snyderman, B. (1959). *The motivation to work.* New York, NY: Wiley.
Maslow, A. H. (1987). *Motivation and personality* (3rd ed.). New York, NY: HarperCollins. (Original work published 1954)
McConaughy, J. L. (1918). The worship of the yardstick. *Educational Review, 55,* 191–192.
McGregor, D. (1960). *The human side of enterprise.* New York, NY: McGraw-Hill.
Norton, M. S., Kelly, L. K., & Battle, A. R. (2012). *The principal as student advocate: A guide for doing what's best for all students.* Larchmont, NY: Eye on Education.
Taylor, F. W. (1911). *Scientific management.* New York, NY: Harper & Row.
Tead, O., & Metcalf, H. C. (1920). *Personnel administration.* New York, NY: McGraw-Hill.
Urwick, L., & Gulick, L. (Eds.). (1937). *Papers on the science of administration.* New York, NY: Columbia University, Institute of Public Administration.
Vroom, V. H. (1964). *Work and motivation.* New York, NY: Wiley.

Chapter 3

Teaching and Learning: Promoting Student Achievement

Primary chapter goal: To discuss how humans learn and the many factors and conditions that influence effective or ineffective teaching and learning results for students.

This chapter centers on student learning. How do human beings learn? What conditions influence effective learning results? What about the importance of learning styles? What are some of the important theories that help us foster learning for all students? Do classroom conditions have anything to do with learning? How can the school principal best support the learning culture of his or her school? Why is it of primary importance that educational supervisors be knowledgeable of the answers to these questions? The answers to just one of these questions could constitute a complete chapter of this book. We have selected the major topic of learning theories for inclusion in this chapter. How humans learn, learning styles of students, and several related applications of learning theories are discussed.

THEORY IS ULTIMATELY TRANSFORMED INTO PRACTICE

How might you reply to an individual who told you that theory in the end is the most practical of all things? After all, the common view of theory is that it is someone's guess about something that has never been proven. It was John Dewey (1929), an educational thinker, who stated this truth. Basic research and theory are essential for creative leadership on the part of educational leaders. Theory provides a framework from which a supervisor can describe behavior and guide his or her services. Theory is ultimately transformed into what we often term best practice.

Viable theory establishes a basic way for the supervisor to define and analyze a problem by providing a framework from which to gather facts and information. A theory serves as a means of generating ideas and predicting outcomes. A theoretical premise serves as a foundation for extending knowledge and understanding. From this foundation new theories can be generated, thus extending an evolutionary flow of information. It serves as a way for the supervisor to perceive and interpret a situation facing him or her. It provides a rich foundation for not only understanding but also from which to establish practices and make decisions based on insight as opposed to guesswork. Such knowledge serves as the foundation for services that must be provided by the supervisor of instruction in a school setting.

HANLON'S THEOREM 21

Theory helps us to better understand behaviors such as motivation, engagement, and initiative. Hanlon (1968) expressed the view that human motivation was released in proportion to situational ego involvement. That is, a person will act on the basis of task involvement in a positive or negative direction. That is, he or she will join an organization or patronize a particular store or become an unhappy worker from an activity perspective, but he or she will not become a creative, efficient worker either for or against a "cause" unless he or she sees himself or herself as personally involved.

Figure 3.1 models Theorem 21. Right of center, the perception is that of task involvement whereby energy is directed toward compliance. At the left of center perceived task involvement releases energy but in a negative spirit of opposition. Moving farther from center in either direction, personal involvement increases in support or in opposition depending on how the matter centers on one's ideals. The more the individual perceives the situation as advancing toward personal goals (ideals), the more energy is released in the direction of aid or support. If the individual wishes to call forth the highest creative energies, he or she must be persuaded that oriented goals are at stake.

The crux of the matter is if the supervisor is to call forth the highest creative energy for the organization, he or she must persuade all members that the situation at hand does indeed involve the organization's members at their highest level of their oriented goals.

If the supervisor or school leader is to call forth the highest levels of creative energy for the organization, he or she must persuade all school personnel that the situation does in fact involve the highest ideals for organizational members. They must be ego involved. Goals must be kept continuously in mind in the midst of ever-changing conditions. It would appear that Hanlon's Theorem 21 would not only be important for motivational purposes

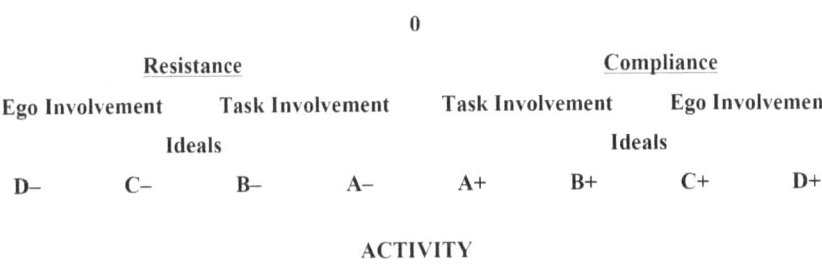

Figure 3.1 Hanlon's Theorem 21

in education but for other groups such as sports teams and business and industrial organizations.

HOW HUMANS LEARN: COGNITIVE LEARNING

Cognitive learning is viewed as using what we know to gain new knowledge. We do this through perception and thinking. It includes reasoning, intuition, and using prior experience. It results from the individual's listening, observing, and experiencing. In the following section, several cognitive learning theories are summarized. For a supervisor to truly be effective, he or she must be knowledgeable of how humans learn; viable learning theories loom important in this respect. To assume that all individuals learn in the same way is contrary to the fact that individuals differ.

Bloom's Taxonomy

Bloom and colleagues (1956), among other authorities, believe that the widely accepted framework of Bloom's taxonomy should be used by all teachers to guide students through the cognitive learning process. As pointed out by Sergiovanni and Starratt (1983), "By observing the questioning patterns of teachers in an instructional setting, one can see whether the teacher is focusing on simple recall or memory of terms or whether he or she is asking for more. All too often, teachers test for memory only and seldom go beyond that to require students to think" (p. 251). Supervisors should look for specific evidence that the teacher is encouraging student learning by delving deeper into the upper learning levels of understanding, analysis, and application. Bloom's taxonomy sets forth six levels of human learning from low to high: remembering, understanding, applying, analyzing, evaluating, and creating.

A student's level of learning is revealed in his or her ability to answer questions related to levels of understanding from simple remembering to high levels of analyzing, evaluating, and then creating. For example, such activities as recognizing, repeating, and memorizing serve to enhance remembering, the lower level of the learning pyramid (see Figure 3.2). To assess and foster the next learning level of the pyramid, that of understanding, questions related to describing, explaining, and discussing the concept are used. As learning is increased the learning levels of evaluating and creating come into play. For evaluating, questions focus on choosing, comparing, valuing, and other assessing questions: How would you check your answer to that fraction division problem, Tommy? What evidence would you cite, Mary, to support your science experiment results?

Piaget's Constructivism

Inhelder and Piaget (1958) set forth the concept of "how we come to know" and the stages a human goes through as he or she acquires this ability. Piaget's work was initiated because of his interest in learning how children think. In brief, Piaget hypothesized that a child's cognitive development depended on his or her biological development, experience with the physical environment, experience with the social environment, and equilibrium. Equilibrium is viewed as a balance between the mental representation of perceptions of ideas and one's external environment.

The implications of cognitive theory models for the supervisor are based on the beliefs that a student's intellectual ability to think logically occurs in stages according to age and experience. Thus, supervisors encourage the teacher to provide a wide range of resource materials and a variety of learning experiences using mental, physical, and social experiences that extend the student's personal interests and knowledge. For example, group work activities, peer tutoring, and informal class activities can extend social relationships. Mobility, health, touch, and use of the senses constitute aspects of physical experiences. Mental experiences are ongoing in the daily learning exercises related to such applications as Bloom's taxonomy.

Situated Cognition

Situated cognition is a theory that posits that knowing is inseparable from doing, inseparable from context, activity, people, culture, and language (Wikipedia, 2015). The concept views learning in terms of the student's performance growth across experiences as opposed to the storing of knowledge. Humans develop meanings through interacting in various aspects of practices within communities. Individuals learn through experiences with the tools, technologies, and languages given by sociocultural groups.

Bloom's Taxonomy

Highest Level

6. *Creating* (*Composing*)—Reading and studying the available research on student retention in grade and then authoring an article on the topic for possible publication in a professional journal, completing a thorough study of the literature, observing the affective and cognitive characteristics of effective teachers, and then designing a test that is 95 percent reliable in identifying teachers that will be highly effective in the classroom

5. *Evaluating* (*Synthesis*)—Listening to a candidate's speech and pointing out consistencies and inconsistencies in his or her remarks, listening to several proposals for solving the immigration problems in the country and then choosing the one that is believed to be the best solution by stating reasons and evidence for the choice

4. *Analyzing* (*Analysis*)—Reading a newspaper report and showing which statements are based on fact and which are based on opinion, comparing gas prices among several states and accounting for variations

3. *Applying* (*Application*)—Using a road map to determine the shortest route from one place to another, writing a paper showing why you believe a student locker search violates the First Amendment of the U.S. Constitution

2. *Understanding* (*Comprehension*)—Showing the population increases on a graph, reading a poem and restating it in one's own words

1. *Remembering* (*Knowledge*)—Defining, listing state capitols, naming U.S. presidents

Lowest Level

Figure 3.2 Bloom's Taxonomy for Learning

The volume of studies and articles on the topic of situated cognition extends far beyond the scope of this chapter. Nevertheless, its implications for student learning are important for learning leaders in school communities. Authorities such as Gibson (1979); Brown, Collins, and Duguid (1989); Wilson (2002); Eysenck and Keane (2005); and many other researchers should be read and studied for further understanding of this learning concept. Several key principles are associated with situated cognition related to memory, knowing, learning, perception, and language. The learning principle, for example, gives one the importance of being knowledgeable of situated cognition.

Because knowing is rooted in action and cannot be decontextualized from individual, social, and historical goals, teaching approaches that focus on conveying facts and rules separately from the contexts within which they are meaningful in real life do not allow for learning that is based on the detection of invariants. They are therefore considered to be impoverished methods that are unlikely to lead to transfer. Learning must involve more than the transmission of knowledge but must instead encourage the expression of effectiveness and the development of attention and inattention through rich contexts that reflect real-life learning processes (Wikipedia, 2015).

HOW HUMANS LEARN: LEARNER-CENTERED THEORIES

Multiple Intelligence and Learning Styles

Multiple intelligence theory contends that there are eight intelligences that all human beings possess in varying degrees (Giles, Pitre, & Womack, 2003). In addition, each individual has a different intelligence profile, and education can be improved by assessing a student's profile and providing experiences accordingly. Each intelligence is found in different parts of the brain; the eight intelligences might operate together or independently, and the eight intelligences tend to define the human species.

Giles and others (2003) underscored the primary importance of the multiple intelligence theory by stating that

> although the theory was not originally designed for use in a classroom application, it has been widely embraced by educators. . . . Teachers have always known that students had different strengths and weaknesses in the classroom. . . . Teachers were encouraged to begin to think of lesson planning in terms of meeting the needs of a variety of the intelligences. (p. 4)

The Eight Intelligences

A thought-provoking concept relating to individual differences among human beings, as just discussed, is that of *intelligences*. The often stated concept that students are different is underscored by the following information:

1. Verbal-Linguistic Intelligence is the ability to understand and manipulate words and languages.

2. Logical-Mathematical Intelligence is the ability to do things with data, use inductive and deductive logic, solve mathematical problems, and see patterns and relationships.
3. Visual-Spatial Intelligence is the ability to form and manipulate a mental model.
4. Bodily-Kinesthetic Intelligence is the ability to process information through the sensations felt in the body.
5. Naturalistic Intelligence recognizes and classifies plants, animals, and minerals including a mastery of taxonomies.
6. Musical Intelligence understands, creates, and interprets musical pitches, timbre, rhythm, and tones and the ability to compose music.
7. Interpersonal Intelligence is the ability to interpret and respond to moods, emotions, motivations, and actions of others.
8. Intrapersonal Intelligence is the ability to know oneself and be aware of one's own strengths and weaknesses.

Giles and others (2003) authored an excellent article on multiple intelligences that sets forth the strengths, preferences, learning best arrangements, and needs of each of the eight intelligences. For example, students with mathematical-logical intelligence possess the strengths of math, logic, problem solving, reasoning, and patterns. They prefer to question, work with numbers, experiment, and solve problems. They learn best through working with relationships and patterns, classifying, categorizing, and working with the abstract. These students need things to think about and explore, science/manipulative materials, and trips to places where math and science are observable. The point emphasized by the foregoing concept is clear. If educators really believe that students differ, then our teaching and learning methods must differ for individual students as well.

TEACHING AND LEARNING IN THE AFFECTIVE DOMAIN

Empirical and basic research findings have underscored the fact that affective characteristics are important in the teaching and learning process. The ways that teachers relate to students and react to them in the classroom can enhance or inhibit the outcomes of student achievement and positive behavior. Both affective and cognitive characteristics of teachers reflect positively in the teaching performance of great teachers. As noted by Hunt (2015), "The synthesis concludes that it is clearly evident that affective factors are an important dimension of the teaching/learning process and that the ways in which teachers respond to students and classroom situations relate to cognitive outcomes such as achievement and behavior" (p. 1).

Norton (2015) completed a comprehensive review of the literature in relation to characteristics of high-quality teachers. The results of that survey are included in Figure 3.3. (Note that the listed number of entries represents the number of times a particular characteristic was included in the various reports and studies reviewed. Thus, the information is not presented as a scientific study but rather as a display of the many characteristics of effective teachers as viewed by various individuals and research groups.) Note that the seventeen characteristics listed in the figure were the leading characteristics of fifty-six others found in the review of literature.

Numerous other related learning theories have been set forth historically. It would take volumes to detail this literature. Inquiry strategies, tools for teaching and learning, socially oriented theories, direct instruction strategies, and inquiry strategies are prominent. We have selected some of these learning theory topics for discussion in this chapter: tools for teaching and learning, socially oriented theories, and inquiry strategies. Each of these learning concepts underscores the importance of knowledge that will serve the school principal and other personnel in their efforts to improve their supervisory competence.

Teacher Characteristics	*Affective Characteristics*	*Cognitive Characteristics*
Teacher Knowledge, Test Scores		11 entries
High Expectations/Standards/Goals		9 entries
Preparation/Credentials		7 entries
Caring/Loving	4 entries	
Classroom Climate	4 entries	
Communication skills	4 entries	
Enthusiasm	3 entries	
Student Achievement Gains		3 entries
Is Organized		3 entries
Effective Teaching Strategies		3 entries
Skillful Teaching, Knows Teaching		2 entries
Monitors Student Learning		2 entries
Motivates Students		2 entries
Is Fair	2 entries	
Has Sense of Humor	2 entries	
Meets Student Needs		2 entries
Is a Good Listener	2 entries	

Figure 3.3 Leading Affective and Cognitive High-Quality Teacher Characteristics

Tools for Teaching and Learning

Cognitive apprenticeship includes such concepts as scaffolding, metacognition, and schema theory. *Scaffolding* refers to techniques that structure learning such as outlines and questions used to form a framework for further learning. Consider the situation whereby a student is unable to understand how to move ahead on a particular skill needed to multiply numbers with decimals. The teacher might break down the task by reviewing multiplication with whole numbers, moving to a problem with only the multiplicand having one decimal point, and then moving to a more complex decimal problem with decimal numbers of both the multiplicand and multiplier. Or, perhaps a teacher might break up a learning experience into appropriate parts and then give the student assistance in learning each part. Beginning with a simplified part of a lesson and providing help with an increasingly more complex aspect of the lesson is one example of scaffolding.

When a student is unable to read at the required level needed for a class project, the teacher might provide help with the appropriate vocabulary, use only one excerpt of the required reading for developing understanding, and give other mini lessons that move the student upward toward the level of reading required in the lesson at hand. By explaining the purposes of a lesson, providing step-by-step procedures for completing the lesson, and showing how the lesson builds on what students have "mastered" previously, the new lesson will be less frustrating to the student and more likely to be achieved.

Metacognition refers to a student's awareness of his or her mental processes. Awareness is critical to planning, goal setting, assessment of content, and monitoring for understanding. *Schema theory* is based on the concept that existing understandings set the stage for the way new knowledge is perceived; the concept can become quite complex. For our purposes, the concept is viewed as a way of extending one's learning from what is already known. Because what the student already knows might be incorrect, it is the goal of the teacher to either correct the misunderstanding or expand learning on the basis of what is known. The concept includes the strategy of helping the student organize their thinking in preparation for expanding what is known.

Reviewing prior lessons or material that supports the expansion of what is known is a good strategy. Or the teacher might ask questions, such as "What do you know about linear equations in mathematics?" and have each student write down his or her answers. Listing the student's answers on the board might provide a foundational basis for moving ahead to quadratic equations. Perhaps the English teacher says, "Let's review what we have learned about the objective case and the nominative case before introducing the proper use of 'I' or 'me' in prepositional phrases."

Authorities in the field strongly recommend that teachers use the schema concept in the classroom. It is argued that the most important consideration when using schema theory is to make certain that a student's existing schemas are up and running at a conscious level (East Tennessee State University, 2001). *Semantic mapping* is another technique used to help students tap into their prior knowledge and expand on this knowledge through vocabulary development.

Metacognition refers to a student's awareness of his or her mental processes. Awareness is critical to planning, goal setting, assessing content, and monitoring for understanding. Wilson (2002) called metacognition the gift that keeps giving. In this author's words, "Students who succeed academically often rely on being able to think effectively and independently in order to take charge of their own learning" (p. 1). Students who are successful with metacognition concepts are viewed as being well organized, keeping work on schedule, planning their learning activities, monitoring their learning progress, and recognizing the time for which change in procedures is necessary.

Wilson (2002) recommends several ways in which teachers can foster metacognition on the part of their students: (1) helping students give serious thought to how they can become better learners, (2) asking students to describe the benefits of driving their brains well, (3) letting students decide what they want to read and what topics they would like to know more about, (4) looking for opportunities to discuss metacognition and point out ways in which it is being utilized, and (5) having teachers use metacognition in problem solving themselves (pp. 1–2).

A CHANGE OF PACE: FLUNKING GRADES AND STUDENT LEARNING

The preceding chapter's discussion should serve to underscore the fact that we all talk about the fact that students are different. One thing is for certain: Students learn differently and at different levels and speeds. We all have heard or read about the historical one-room schoolhouse. Students in grades 1 through 8 typically were housed in the same room with the same teacher. As town and city populations grew, the number of students in a community increased as well. The one-room schoolhouse became outmoded and more schools with more rooms were needed. But what about the placement of students? The answer was to group students according to age and place students of age five in first grade, age six in second grade, age seven in third grade, and so forth. But what about the achievement differences of students? How is this to be handled? The answer: Just promote the gifted student to a higher grade and retain the slow learner in the same grade for one more year.

Although we have progressed to some extent in regard to student retention, student failure in grades remains in place nationally. In the long run, grade retention is one of the leading factors of student dropout rates. A high student dropout rate is unsatisfactory for a country that is based on a democracy. As Thomas Jefferson stated, "If a nation expects to be ignorant and free in a state of civilization, it expects what never was and never will be." However, retention in grades remains a serious problem in our schools nationally. Government pressures at the federal and state levels have set forth standards that militate against the efforts to actually meet the verbal statement of "failure is not an option." The topic of student retention is discussed in the following section primarily because of its influence on student academic achievement and student dropouts.

Myths Regarding Student Retention and Academic Performance

A third-grade student has not "mastered" the subject matter standards for grade 3. For him or her to gain in academic performance, it is best to retain him or her in third grade for another year. True or false? The volume of research on this subject has made it quite clear that the student will learn more if being allowed to enter grade 4 than if retained in the same grade. As noted by Shepard and Smith (1989), "The meta-analysis of the sixty-three studies is consistent with previous reviews of research and earlier meta-analysis finding largely negative effects of retention. On average, retained children are worse off than their promoted counterparts on both adjustment and academic outcomes" (p. 27). The finding of "worse off" applies to the level of academic performance, behavior and social traits, and future success experiences. In addition, as previously mentioned, failing a grade is one primary characteristic of later school dropouts. Performance standards and improvements in education once again have become foremost in the minds of national leaders because of education's influence on the national economy. We are fully aware of the arguments set forth in favor of "getting tough on student retention" and the major faults of social promotion. We submit, however, that these contentions have been challenged and proven to be flawed by numerous research studies and empirical practices.

It is clear that *if* student academic achievement is truly the primary goal of schooling, failing students in grade must be abolished. Alternatives to flunking students is something that intelligent educators can implement. Local control of such needs is imperative for reaching a best solution to the problem of student retention.

Proof Beyond Any Doubts

If we really want to improve student learning and overall the education of the nation's children and youth, minimally four myths must be countered. Myth number 1 is that student retention in grade ensures mastery of subject matter, myth number 2 is that retention is one way to help students have more time to grow and mature, myth number 3 is that retention serves to reduce the range of abilities in classes and therefore places pupils closer to their peers in relation to learning, and myth number 4 is that retention serves as a motivational factor to pupils—it awakens the unmotivated pupil and serves to remove his or her apathy.

Both empirical and basic research, however, make it clear that each of the foregoing beliefs is flawed (Norton, 1983). Non-promotion does not increase learning; rather pupils who are retained learn less than pupils of like ability who are promoted. Non-promotion does not increase socialization or learning readiness; retained pupils often show regression. Non-promotion does not increase the homogeneity of groups; retained children tend to choose companions from grades higher than their own and socialization is not improved. Non-promotion does not lead to improving the pupil's attitude and behavior. It tends to promote discipline problems, is a negative influence on the child's self-concept, and serves as a factor for becoming a future school dropout. Early studies by Sowards and Scobey (1961), Dobbs and Neville (1967), Gaite (1969), Street and Leigh (1971), Godfrey (1972), Reiter (1973), White and Howards (1973), Cunningham and Owens (1976), Koons (1977), Bocks (1977), Shepard and Smith (1989), and other authorities have pointed out clearly the negative results of flunking grades.

Recommendations for Eliminating Student Retention

The best way to curtail student retention is to educate school leaders, teachers, and parents of the history of retention and its negative effects on students. Both parents and teachers are not correctly informed about the results of pupil retention. Ill-informed teachers who retain students attempt to persuade parents of the benefits of retention as soon as their children are at risk. Parents tend to become convinced that retention is best for their children through such comments that they comply because of the "fear" of consequences (Shepard & Smith, 1989). Providing students with merely "more of the same," whether retained or promoted, is unlikely to produce positive outcomes.

A team approach to the problems of remediation of learning difficulties is essential. Special concern must be given to causes of learning problems through special diagnosis and then prescriptions drafted based on collective judgments of the members of the student's educational team. Merely eliminating social promotion will not solve the problem. Programs that were inappropriate for failing students the first time are likely to be equally inappropriate and of less interest to the student a second time. Effective remediation, tutoring, peer tutoring, parental help programs, and other forms of cooperative learning have many benefits for the deficient student. Empirical evidence has shown that the practice of cross-age or peer tutoring whereby a second grader who is behind in math shows learning gains for both the target student and the student tutor.

Alternative instructional arrangements that provide for differing learning progress can be instrumental in encouraging student success as well as serving as a positive vehicle for motivating at-risk students to remain in school. Ungraded types of school organization can serve to remove the stigma of grade retention while allowing for instruction at the success level of the student. The basic concept of cognitive learning, previously discussed, comes into play in this regard. That is, learning is not viewed as a "building blocks" process whereby step-by-step linear learning takes place. Cognitive learning, on the other hand, views learning from constructs more like a "Tinkertoy." That is, learning involves making connections between the learner's existing network and knowledge of new information that is learned at a later time. When what is already known and the new knowledge are connected, insight takes place.

Of course, the preceding information is a simplified explanation of a far more complex concept. In addition, contemporary thinking relative to standards-based learning and human intelligences looms important when considering student academic performance and individual differences in all learners. In the final analysis, it is the classroom teacher who has the greatest knowledge of the student's achievement, and for this reason teachers should be the first people concerned with the student's success and what should be done to correct related learning problems.

THE EFFECTS OF CLASSROOM PHYSICAL PHENOMENA ON STUDENT LEARNING

Thoughts concerning effective learning commonly focus on teacher competency, school principal leadership, effective supervisory practices, and other affective and cognitive factors. However, many "studies" contend that physical conditions within the classroom also have positive or negative influences on student learning. Although we have never heard of a teacher who requested that his or her classroom be painted blue, we wouldn't be surprised if this has actually happened. The color blue reportedly serves as a calming effect on student behavior.

We have wondered about the thinking of school supervisors concerning the effects of color, space, seating, lighting, distance communication, and other physical factors on student behavior and learning, if any. The literature is replete with information on the effects of the foregoing physical factors on effective learning. For example, Rendeiro (2012) contends that "lighting influences everything from blood pressure to mood to ability to concentrate" (p. 1). Dinsmore (2016) states, "The effects of color on learning are well documented, and it is important that when choosing a color for your classroom, you keep in mind the powerful effects these decisions can have on young learners" (p. 1).

An article posted by Professional Learning Board (2016) reported that seating arrangements affect the learning process (p. 1). Although it seems important that one read information regarding the effects of various design factors on student learning, it also is necessary for personnel to differentiate a reliable study from a company advertisement. The following sections point out how lighting, color, seating arrangements, temperature, building conditions, aesthetic surroundings, and other physical factors can effect what a student learns. We present the following information with some concern relative to the extent that effective research supports certain claims. In any case, color and other physical factors have been reported by many writers as having direct effects on student learning in the classroom. For example, Tanner (1999) reported on thirty different studies that focused on the effects of color, lighting, and other physical factors on student learning.

Classroom Colors

Blue and purple colors have been found to have a calming effect on learners and thus might serve a positive purpose for lessening tension in classrooms or in classes with emotionally disturbed children and those with attention deficit disorder or attention deficit, and attention and hypertension disorder. Red colors have been found to increase the heart rate and interfere with the ability to learn. Black and brown colors have been associated with anxiety. Dinsmore (2016) states that black and white colors, with their stark contrasts, have been shown to lower the IQ of students in the classroom. The author does not provide a reliable reference to support this contention. Sasson (2009) set forth the belief that a light shade of teal green is reenergizing and acts as a gentle reminder of spring to come, making the middle semester more bearable and interesting, thus creating a calmer learning atmosphere.

Noise Hinders How Children Learn

Our interest in school climate and effective student learning does not appear to focus on the foregoing factors. After all, teachers and administrators commonly have little influence on such building facility matters; that is up to the building maintenance crew. We submit that such concerns are of paramount importance for those leaders responsible for effective student learning. Give thought to a recent research concerning the negative effects of noise on a child's learning. According to research by the American Association for the Advancement of Science, "one of the worst offenders when a child's trying to listen is other voices babbling in the background" (Neergaard, 2016, p. 11A).

According to reports by several medical authorities, the cacophony of day care to the buzz of TV and electric toys, noise is more distracting to a child's brain than an adult's. New research makes it clear that it can hinder how youngsters learn. Dr. Rochelle Leibold of Boys Town National Research Hospital in Omaha, Nebraska, points out that research has implications for classroom design. For example, the type of flooring or ceiling height can either soften kids' natural noise or bounce it around (Neergaard, 2016).

Should supervisors give thought and attention to the foregoing sections relating to physical phenomena and student learning? There certainly appears to be sufficient evidence that they should do so. Those leaders that are responsible for school building design and maintenance also must be knowledgeable of valid and reliable studies related to physical factors that foster or inhibit student learning in schools and the classroom. What about a walk-through observation of those factors that contribute to or distract from effective student learning in your school's classrooms? What about the noise factors inside and outside the classrooms? According to Dr. Rochelle Newman of the University of Maryland, if someone coughs or a car horn blares, it can drown out part of a word or sentence. An adult's brain can usually fill in the missing word, but a young child does not do this. Check the lighting influences. Are outside automobile noises interfering with a child's ability to learn?

KEY IDEAS AND RECOMMENDATIONS

- Supervisors to be of real help to teachers must be highly knowledgeable on the topic of how students learn. Basing supervisory services on "here's how I do it" is ineffective. Helping the teacher to know, understand, and implement viable theories of good practice serves the primary foundation for improved practice.
- Contrary to the beliefs of many, theory is the most practical of all things. Its value lies in its serving as a framework for describing human behavior, gathering factual information, and implementing best practices.
- Cognitive learning centers on gaining new knowledge through such strategies as informed questioning techniques that increase thinking on the part

of the student. A variety of cognitive theory is available for supervisors and teachers to use relative to revealing differences in student learning intelligences and styles.
- Situated learning is based on the concept that knowing is inseparable from doing. Interacting experientially is an important factor for increasing learning opportunities.
- It is a must that supervisors and teachers be highly knowledgeable of the research that has been completed on variances in student intelligences. The common statement that students are different reaches far beyond the fact that maturity and the basic intelligence of students differ. Variances in intelligence include, according to theory, the fact that some humans have strong brain variances relative to music, mathematics, language, and other subject areas.
- Affective characteristics loom important in relation to student learning. The ways in which teachers respond to students inhibit or foster learning results. Such affective characteristics as caring, fairness, enthusiasm, and communication affect student–teacher relationships and in turn student achievement.
- Building more effective lesson plans and improved student learning are enhanced by using such learning tools as scaffolding, metacognition, schema theory, and others. Supervisors must be professionally prepared to help teachers implement these building tools in their classrooms.
- It is clear that retaining students in grades has no benefits for learning or behavior improvements for the student. Volumes of reliable research have shown that retention militates against learning performance, improvements in social behavior, self-esteem, and motivation for continued learning.

Discussion

1. Assume the role of a school principal who is visiting with one of your teachers about engaging students in the learning process. Briefly outline one of the theories discussed in the chapter related to the matter at hand. Write a brief paragraph on the main points that you would discuss with the teacher. How would you suggest that the teacher initiate this procedure?
2. The topic of individual intelligences of human beings is presented in some depth in the chapter. Review the information on this topic and then write a paragraph on just how you have observed this concept in your personal experiences.
3. Assume that you are about to initiate a new unit/lesson on a specific lesson in mathematics, English grammar, or other subject that you

prefer. Briefly explain how you might use the technique of semantic mapping, scaffolding, or schema theory to introduce the instruction.
4. Give some thought to the recommendations set forth in this chapter concerning the importance of theory in the work of the supervisor. On a scale of 1 (low) to 10 (high), to what extent have you observed the implementation of theoretical constructs in your professional experience in teaching or administrative activities? Take a few minutes to answer the question, "Why is your rating on the scale as low, high, or otherwise rated on the scale?"
5. Student retention was discussed in depth in this chapter. Take a few minutes to discuss your views with another appropriate educator or write a brief paragraph on your philosophy regarding student retention.

CASE STUDY

Case 3.1: With All Due Respect

Sara Oliva, a new principal at Wymore Elementary School, is meeting after school for the first time with the faculty. After commenting on her good feelings about the opportunity to work with the school faculty, she comments about her wishes to work with them during the year on two major objectives. First, Miss Oliva states that she hopes that Wymore could become an inclusive school whereby every student was able to succeed by experiencing a program of instruction on the basis of his or her personal interests and needs.

"Secondly," says Miss Oliva, "I want each of us at Wymore to become a true student advocate. This means that we view things from the student's perspective, stand up for students' rights and concerns, be good listeners, create an environment in which each student can focus on their personal interests and beliefs, and make decisions that are always in the best interests of our students."

At that point, Alex Moreno raises his hand and is recognized by principal Oliva.

"With due respect," says Alex, "Your purposes are worthy but, in my opinion, impossible to implement. With twenty-seven sixth graders in my classroom, meeting the special interests and needs of each one of them is nothing more than high hopes. The social, physical, and mental behaviors of these students widely differ. And, again, about half of the class members apparently do not come to school to learn. I know that I can teach what the state and school officials want me to teach, but I can't guarantee that the pupils will learn it or even want to learn it."

Principal Oliva observes the heads of most faculty members in attendance shaking in agreement.

Discussion

1. Assume the role of Principal Oliva. How might you respond on the spot to Alex Moreno's comments? Avoid "brushing off" the comments by saying, "We will have to discuss that situation and deal with it as we can." Or, "What do others of you think we have to do to resolve this problem?" Rely on the chapter's information relative to cognitive learning, student engagement, affective characteristics of effective teachers, or even appropriate theories discussed in the previous chapter.

REFERENCES

Bloom, B. S., Engelhart, M. D., Furst, E. J., Hill, W. H., & Krathwohl, D. R. (1956). *Taxonomy educational objectives; The classification of educational goals. Handbook I: Cognitive domain.* New York, NY: Davis McKay Company.

Bocks, W. M. (1977, February). Non-promotion: A year to grow. *Educational Leadership,* 379–383.

Brown, J. S., Collins, A., & Duguid, P. (1989). A neuropsychological interpretation response to Vera Simon. *Cognitive Science, 17,* 87–116.

Cunningham, W. G., & Owens, R. C. (1976). Social promotion: Problem or solution? *NASSP Bulletin, 60,* 25–29.

Dewey, J. (1929). *Sources of a science of education.* New York, NY: Liveright.

Dinsmore, K. (2016, January 30). *The best paint color for classroom walls.* Retrieved from http://www.ehowcom/way--616--paint-color-classsroom-walls.html.

Dobbs, V., & Neville, D. (1967, July–August). The effects of non-promotion on the achievement of groups matched from retained first graders and promoted second graders. *Journal of Educational Research, 60,* 472–475.

East Tennessee University. (2001, January). *Schema theory: What is a schema?* Retrieved from www.etsu.edu/fsi/learning/schematheory.apsx

Eysenck, M. W., & Keane, M. T. (2005). *Cognitive psychology* (5th ed.). New York, NY: Psychology Press.

Gaite, A. J. H. (1969, May). *On the validity of non-promotion as an educational procedure.* Madison, WI: University of Wisconsin Press.

Gibson, J. J. (1979). *The ecological approach to visual perception.* Boston, MA: Houghton Mifflin.

Giles, E., Pitre, S., & Womak, S. (2003). Multiple intelligences and learning styles. In M. Orey (Ed.), *Emerging perspectives on learning, teaching and technology.* Retrieved from http://epltt.coe.uga.edu/

Godfrey, M. L. (1972). The tragedy of failure. *Education Digest, 37,* 34–35.

Hanlon, J. M. (1968). *Administration and education.* Belmont, CA: Wadsworth.

Hunt, W. C. (2015, December 31). *Teaching and learning in the affective domain: A review of the literature.* Retrieved from http://eric.ed.lgovb/?id=ED288871

Inhelder, B., & Piaget, J. (1958). *The growth of logical thinking from childhood to adolescence.* New York, NY: Basic Books.

Koons, C. L. (1977). Non-promotion: A dead-end road. *Phi Delta Kappan, 58*(9), 701–702.

Neergaard, L. (2016, February 15). Noise hinders how children learn. *Arizona Republic,* p. 11A.

Norton, M. S. (1983). It's time to get tough on student promotion—Or is it? *Contemporary Education, 54*(4), 283–286.

Norton, M. S. (2015). *Teacher with the magic: Great teachers change students' lives.* Lanham, MD: Rowman & Littlefield.

Professional Learning Board. (2016). *Do seating arrangements have an impact on student learning?* Retrieved from http://k12teacherstaffdevelopment.com/tlb/do-seating-arrangements-have-an-impact-on-student-learning/

Reiter, R. G. (1973). *The promotion/retention dilemma: What research tells us.* Report No. 7416. Philadelphia, PA: Philadelphia School District.

Rendeiro, M. F. (2012, May 24). *The effects of classroom lighting on learning.* Retrieved from http://www.united-academics.org/health-medicine/the-effects-of-classroom-lighting-on-learning/

Sergiovanni, T. J., & Starratt, R. J. (1983). *Supervision: Human perspectives.* New York, NY: McGraw-Hill Book Company.

Shepard, L. A., & Smith. M. L. (1989). *Flunking grades: Research and policies on retention.* Philadelphia, PA: The Falmer Press.

Sinofsky, E. R., & Knirck, F. G. (1981). Choose the right color for your learning style. *Instructional Innovator, 26*(3), 17–19.

Sowards, G. W., & Scobey, M. M. (1961). *The changing curriculum and the elementary teacher.* San Francisco, CA: Wadsworth Publishing Co.

Street, P., & Leigh, T. M. (1971, March). Suffer the little Kentucky first-graders. *Bureau of School Services Bulletin,* No. 43.

White, K., & Howards, J. L. (1973, March). Failure to be promoted and self-concept among elementary school children. *Elementary School Guidance and Counseling,* 182–187.

Wikipedia. (2015, December 30). *Situated cognition.* Retrieved from https://en.wikipedia.org/wiki/Situated--cognition.

Wilson, M. (2002). Six views of embodied cognition. *Psychonomic Bulletin and Review, 9*(4), 625–636.

Chapter 4

Determining Learning Standards

Primary chapter goal: To examine standards-based learning in relation to its surrounding controversies and probable future.

LEARNING STANDARDS FOR STUDENTS: WHO IS TO DECIDE? WHAT SHOULD BE EMPHASIZED?

Learning standards center on what school students are to know, understand, and be able to do. But who is to decide on what standards are to be established? In addition, what should be the nature of learning standards? Abbott (2014) states, "Learning standards describe educational objectives—i.e., what students should have learned by the end of a course, grade level, or grade span—but they do not describe any particular teaching practice, curriculum, or assessment method (although this is a source of ongoing confusion and debate)" (p. 1).

The standards-based debate centers on the differences of opinion as to whether specific school curriculum should be established by local, state, or federal agencies; what is to be taught and how it is to be taught. Should a state's learning standards just set forth the educational goals regarding what students should have learned after a period of specified time and leave the curriculum and teaching methods to the local school personnel? In any case who is to decide what standards should be "imposed" on local school curricular programs? However, the standards debate goes beyond which level of government should be the authority for determining the school's curriculum. The debate includes such contentions as whether the curriculum should be focused on learning and work relationships, strictly academic subjects such as math and science, or should it include an equal provision for the fine arts such as music, art, dance, and other emphases such as civics, health and safety, community education, and family living.

The terms *standards-based* and *standards-referenced* need some clarification. When we speak of a standards-based instruction, the focus is on whether students are effectively learning what they are expected to learn as they progress through the school's curriculum. On the other hand, standards-referenced instruction refers to the fact that what students are being taught is tied to learning standards. That is, what is actually being taught to students is based on standards set forth by the state or other resource. Grade reporting for the two concepts is different as well. Traditionally, various student performances are scored (i.e., homework, quizzes, unit tests, projects, final examinations) and averaged for a numerical score that is attached to a grade of A, B, C, and so forth. This form of grading is typical in a standards-referenced course. In a standards-based course, grades revealed are tied to the status of students' progress toward a specific performance standard. Examples of standards-based report cards are presented later in this chapter.

PURPOSE, VISION, MISSION, AND LEARNING STANDARDS

Contemporary school leaders must deal with the purpose, vision, mission, and learning standards of their school; these terms are different but inextricably related. Consider first the questions related to the school's purpose. Principals and their personnel must discuss the questions: Why does our school exist? What are the school's reasons for existing? Whom do we serve? How are our educational purposes determined? As noted by Norton, Kelly, and Battle (2012), there is a subtle difference between "purpose" and "mission." That is, the purpose of the school concerns the "student reasons" for its existence. How does the school go about satisfying its purpose? We recommend that the school *principal and staff first discuss and agree upon how the school is going to go about satisfying its purpose* by asking: What do we stand for? How are we going to serve our students? What are our students' needs and interests? What do we have to do to be certain that we keep our purpose in mind when making learning decisions? The meeting of student needs includes present and future considerations.

The *vision* of the school centers on what the school leader and professional staff consider they want the school to become. This does not mean what will we do in the future; rather it centers on determining what the school must do now to reach its vision for the future. Its *mission* serves to direct the decision-making and problem-solving processes of the school; it clarifies the school principal, professional staff, and school community's views of the goals and planned outcomes of the school's current program (Norton, 2013).

Examples of vision statements might be: "Students that graduate from Union High School will possess the basic knowledge and skills that will prepare them for a variety of career pursuits including preparation for college and careers in various vocational/technical occupations." Or, "Students that complete their course work at Union Elementary School will have the foundational knowledge and skills that will prepare them academically for educational success when entering Union Middle School."

The school's *mission* sets the direction for the school regarding such considerations as college preparatory, vocational/technical orientation, basic skills, or other career pursuits. The mission statement is accompanied by goals, objectives, and standards of achievement. *Goals* represent the primary aims that the school personnel want to accomplish related to the major aim of student learning. *Objectives* lend specific guides toward goal accomplishment.

As previously stated, *standards* are what school students are to know, to understand, and be able to do. The focus of standards-based learning is to increase the assurance that students are gaining the necessary knowledge and skills required for immediate school success, future educational success, and the knowledge and skills required for future work occupations, civic responsibilities, and worthy work–life balances. As Leger (2015) points out, "No test can measure initiative or creativity. . . . But our attitudes toward education would be healthier if we remembered that the fullest measure of its quality can't be known until long after the students graduate" (p. 10A).

STANDARDS-BASED EDUCATION

Standards-based education could be viewed as an extension of previous concepts of competency-based or outcomes-based education. Competency-based education identifies the tasks that are required in a particular subject or area of work and the abilities required to complete the task. The needed required abilities to complete the task are ultimately assessed by *indicators of competency* revealed by the actual behaviors and performances outcomes of the individual.

Relevant standards not only outline what students need to know, understand, and be able to do, but also have the following characteristics and benefits:

- Standards should generally be written so that all students are capable of achieving them, and so that talented students will exceed them.
- All students are believed to be capable of learning and meeting high expectations. Both advanced and slow learners can learn new things in their own way and at their own rates.

- Instruction that helps an individual student learn the information and skills listed in the standards is emphasized.
- Both *excellence* and *equity* are valued. Subgroups are carefully measured to identify and reduce system racism, bias, and the tyranny of low expectations.
- Professional teachers are empowered to make the decisions essential for effective learning, rather than having a teaching style prescribed by an outside group or agency.
- Social promotion is discouraged. Students advance based on their actual learning achievements instead of their age, their friends' achievements, or tradition (Wikipedia, 2016). Note: It seems necessary to explain that in some cases students that do not pass high-stakes testing are denied regular high school diplomas. Rather, a common practice is to give them a certificate of attendance instead.

We recommend other graduation practices and grading systems later in this and other chapters of the book. In any case, we support the practice of having the various states determine the broad categories of curriculum that school districts must provide. In turn, local school boards determine written descriptions of what students are expected to know and be able to do at a specific stage of their education. At that point, the school superintendent and school principals in the school district determine the goals of the particular program courses and then teachers determine how and what to teach students so that they achieve the learning experiences described in the local standards.

Local control of curriculum development is given to the local control of school districts in each state. Students are not held back and are not kept from graduating from high school. Rather, students that have not met expected standards of performance are given a school certificate that shows their levels of attainment and perhaps their class ranking among all class graduates. The future will serve to determine the real ability of each student. See the Snapshot that follows.

SNAPSHOT: THINKING OF STANDARDS-BASED GRADING AND STUDENT TESTING

An issue of the *Arizona Republic* included an article by Robert Leger titled "Real Test of Education Comes Many Years Later" (2015). The author set forth several intriguing points that should make all educators think about students that they have known or even classmates during their high school years. Leger spoke of his class of 1975 reunion and learned that one of his class's top ten students rose to be an Apple vice president. Another member of his graduating class "breezed" through honors classes and now runs five hospitals. Then Leger noted that sometimes potential isn't obvious.

One of his classmates finished in the middle of his 439-student class. After graduation the student enlisted in the Air Force. Ten years later, he retired as a major in intelligence and went on to hold high management positions in two multinational corporations. Leger commented that no single test in high school or perhaps report card grade would have captured whatever it was that gave that former student the discipline and learning that he had realized.

You and most everyone else could name former school classmates that were not viewed as having high academic performance, high-grade report cards, or high potential for future success but have seen these individuals become highly successful contributors to their selected occupations and school communities. This snapshot story certainly gives us reason to pause and think about the dangers of "predicting" potential and even recommending failure for students early in their lives. As Leger suggests, the real test of education comes many years later.

STANDARDS-BASED REPORT CARDS

Many school districts nationally have adopted standards-based report cards in an attempt to reinforce consistent, high expectations for all students and schools. Student-based report cards are designed to accomplish several other objectives including reflecting what a student should know and be able to do at each grade level in all subjects; helping teachers, students, and families focus on the standards throughout the school year; providing specific feedback on progress in the standards so students, families, and teachers can work together to set meaningful goals for improvement; and providing information regarding big ideas and concepts each child has learned and what work is still needed for success in the next grade level (Department of Education, 2016, p. 1).

Those school districts that have adopted standards-based report cards commonly state that the value of the system is revealed in stimulating continuous communication between teachers, parents, and students. In addition, the practice tends to place emphasis on student learning as opposed to just earning a course grade. The process places emphasis on a variety of learning experiences as opposed to one final test or even the grading of several quizzes or unit tests. Learning standards are based on achievement expectations that provide a specific focus for aligning curriculum and instruction and evaluating and assessing these school program processes. The curriculum and supervisory practices are planned and implemented by the local school district in alignment with the state's program standards.

Some school districts' individual schools do give specific letter grades along with other indications of percentage of progress toward a stated performance standard. For example, one teacher stated that she used traditional letter grades but defined them so as to indicate what the grade is intended to mean. For example, a letter grade of A meant that the student completed proficient work on all course objectives and advanced work on some objectives (Sciffiny, 2008). A grade of C meant that the student completed proficient work on most of the important objectives, although not on all objectives. A grade of D meant that the student had completed work on half of the course objectives but was missing some important objectives and is at significant risk of failing the next course in the sequence. A grade of F meant that the student had completed less than half of the course objectives and cannot successfully complete the next course in the sequence. Standards-based report cards measure individual student performance against agreed-on learning standards as opposed to the performance of other students.

There are problems with standards-based report cards as well. Both teachers and parents tend to struggle with the technical difficulties related to aligning instruction and achievement assessment with the new system of reporting. The glitches of new methods of reporting require needs for changes that often result in additional confusion. For example, in some cases the categories in the report card were so numerous that parents were confused about what the report was really telling them. Teachers were troubled in aligning their instruction with the numerous category standards and keeping up with the reporting for each student in their many classes. Just reducing the number of standards/categories does not always resolve teacher and parental concerns.

The use of certain *educationeze* is often troublesome. For example, one school's newsletter stated, "This new report card shows what a child has learned, not what the child has earned." Parents were asking just what the statement really means. One school district introduced a new lettering grade system. The letter M meant that the student meets the standard of understanding information or demonstrating a skill. The letter A meant approaching learning standards, indicating that a student has partial understanding; quite contrary to the meaning of a grade of A historically. Poorly stated communication that is new to parents will always result in confusion and misunderstandings. Frequent "improvements" and changes in traditional practices commonly result in teacher and parental problems.

The formats for student report cards vary but do have common information. Figure 4.1 is an example of a standards-based elementary school report card for a pupil in grade 3. Example 2 reveals a middle school standards-based report card. Both examples have similarities of the more traditional student report cards. The example is not presented as being exemplary, rather as an example that is quite similar to report cards historically.

EXAMPLES OF LEARNING STANDARDS

It is becoming more common for states to delegate the determination of course standards to the local school district. In turn, school boards tend to delegate this important task to the local schools or to a representative committee consisting of district school principals and teachers of the subject/

Example #1 of a Standards-Based Report Card

Wymore Elementary School

Motto: Give Your Best

2075 College View Boulevard   Phone: (480) 100-0000

Pupil Grading Scale   **Skill Level Standards**

A 100-90 %   B 89-80%   C 79-70%   D 69-60%   F 59-0%

Letter Code on Improvement: O-Outstanding, S-Satisfactory, P-Some improvement, N-Needs Improvement

Subjects	Quarters			
	1st	2nd	3rd	4th
Arithmetic	C	B	B	A
Improvement Remarks				
Work effort improvements in evidence, Effort has been outstanding overall	P	S	S	O
Reading/English Spelling	A	A	A	A
Improvement Remarks				
High quality of work each quarter, Is well prepared for future work	O	O	O	O
Social Studies	B	B	B	B
Improvement Remarks				
Homework assignment not always prepared	S	S	S	S
Fine Arts	C	C	C	C
Improvement Remarks				
Quiz results regarding notable artists and famous artworks needs improvement	P	P	P	P
Class attention to instructions would likely result in improved performance	N	N	N	N
Science—Living Things	C	B	B	B
Improvement Remarks				
Early semester performance improvements served well	P	S	S	S

Example #2 of Middle School Standards-Based Report Card

Shadow Mountain Middle School

2075 Laguna Avenue

Lafayette, MT

RECORD OF ATTENDANCE

Term 1		Term 2		Term 3		Term 4	
Assent	Tardy	Absent	Tardy	Absent	Tardy	Absent	Tardy
0	2	1	0				

Grade Report

Course	Task	Term 1	Term 2	Term 3	Term 4
Algebra 1 (G. Lyon)	Final Exam/Project		A		
	Term Grade	A	A		
	Course Grade		A		
	Term 2 Comments: Outstanding performance throughout course				
English 8th (V. Bassett)	Term Grade	A	A		
	Term 2 Comments: Excellent performance throughout course				
Honors Science (R. Mehuron)	Term Grade	A	A		
Social Studies 8th (L. Walker)	Term Grade	A	A		
	Term 2 Comments: Pleasure to have in class				
	Will do well in future social studies classes				
Spanish 2 (C. Henson)		A	A		
	Term 2 Comments: Aural/Oral outstanding				
Student Aide (M. Andrus)	Term Grade	CR	CR		
	Performance Comments: Mentoring was outstanding				

KET

A-Excellent   B-Above Average   C-Average   D-Below Average   F-Failing   CR-credit

Please contact your student's teacher if you have questions about your child's performance in a particular class.

Figure 4.1 Example 1 of a Standards-Based Report Card

course at hand. Perhaps fourth graders are expected to learn equivalent values of fractions and decimal fractions. That is, what decimal fraction is equal to 5/8? Or, which is larger, 3/4 or 2/3? The school standards might require sixth-grade students to know when the nominative and objective cases of personal pronouns are used. For example, which is correct, It is me, or It is I?

Which is correct, Tom and me went to the store, or Tom and I went to the store? Or in the following sentence, which is correct, the fly ball fell to the ground between the right fielder and I, or the fly ball fell to the ground between the right fielder and me?

In an Algebra I course in grade 9, a student might be required to be able to find x in the following linear equation: $4x - 10 = 2x + 30$. A senior high school chemistry student might be required to be quite familiar with the periodic table and know the symbol and atomic number for a chemical such as gold. In any case, although teachers are responsible for teaching the required skills for their students' grade level, the standards should not interfere with teacher creativity by telling how the teacher should teach.

CRITICISMS OF LEARNING STANDARDS

Abbott's (2014) article sets forth six questions of significant importance as related to learning standards. For example, this editor asks the question, "Should states or the federal government determine what students learn in public school?" The arguments are between those that contend that federal government agencies and others need to play a role in setting educational standards to ensure a minimum level of educational quality in public schools and those school representatives that believe that the local school personnel are in the best position to do this task.

The local contingency argues that learning standards established by federal agencies represent a form of governmental overreach and inhibit the historical principle of local control. Another significant question is, "Are learning standards forcing schools and educators to use a mandated curriculum?" Some contend that learning standards set by the federal government are a form of forced curriculum that mandate what teachers can teach and how it is to be taught as exemplified by the Common Core curriculum. The argument that the local school community is in the best position to control what is best for students also is a common contention.

We believe that the most effective curricular decisions for student learning are made by the local school personnel and people within the local school community. A third question posed by Abbott (2014) is, "Are learning standards useful, effective guidelines for schools and educators or are they burdensome regulatory requirements that take up valuable resources and time without adding much educational value?" When properly planned and implemented, learning standards set forth by the states and local school districts can be such that they leave room for discretionary leadership on the part of local school leaders. In turn, teachers are able to use their knowledge, skills, and creative talents in the classroom.

"Do learning standards address the most important and appropriate knowledge and skills?" The answer to this question depends largely on whom you ask. The members of a local school community commonly contend that mandated standards are based on business and other political interests and not on the best interests and needs of students in their communities. The question is asked, "Are learning standards too prescriptive or are they not prescriptive enough?" Teacher autonomy is a problem when top-down requirements are established for what must be taught and how it should be taught.

A final question by Abbott (2014) is, "Do standards represent authentic learning progressions or merely content progressions or teaching progressions?" The question begs for an answer to whether or not school principals are adequately prepared to determine standards for student learning. If so, where is such information acquired? A majority of practicing school principals contends that they are not really prepared to complete such tasks. Thus, the local standards might simply reflect the progressions set forth in a selected mathematics, science, English, or other student textbook.

Although we endorse the use of learning standards, we do not favor the establishment of such standards by the federal government or the intervention of state governments relative to setting forth specific standards that every school must meet or how the various curriculum subjects must be taught. Nevertheless, standards themselves are opposed by various authorities and in many cases by school patrons. The following paragraphs discusses the reasons for such opposition because school leaders at the local level will undoubtedly encounter these opponents.

One major criticism of standards-based learning is related to the emphasis on testing or the dependence on one rigorous test to determine if a student is to obtain a high school diploma. The "cry" is for less testing and more learning in the classroom. Other criticism is directed to such standards claiming that they are not implementing the curricula which follow the new standards (Wikipedia, 2016).

Considerable criticism is directed to standards-based learning because it seems to expect all students to perform at the level of the best students in the classroom; it seems to punish students because they do not perform at the level of the more talented students. The bottom line, however, centers on the opinion that federal and state mandated standards are contrary to the concept of local control of education; they inhibit the initiative and creative leadership of local school districts to meet the special needs of children and youth and restrain the creative abilities of creative teachers.

EXAMPLE OF ONE STATE'S COURSE OF STUDY REQUIREMENTS

One state defined its course of study as being required content for various subjects of kindergarten through grade 8. In doing so, the state board noted that the requirements were to be considered as minimal and that local school boards or teachers were not limited from enriching and enhancing the "minimum course content," but rather encouraged to excel way beyond the basic standards.

Figure 4.2 is an example of how a state might set forth its responsibility for giving direction to curricular offerings at the local level. Such a procedure sets minimal goals and leaves room for local school districts to use their discretion in applying the state's model. In addition, it serves teachers in their attempt to assess the status of a particular student and to provide a meaningful statement regarding a student's progress on a standards-based report card. In addition, such a model could be especially helpful for elementary school teachers that commonly have had only one course in the teaching of mathematics and for supervisors who are planning in-service activities for local school teaching personnel.

The example is not presented as a model that local school districts should implement, but rather as an example of how a state might take the leadership for directing school curriculum without mandating exactly what must be taught or how the subject is to be taught. In addition, local school districts are free to expand the recommended content, for example, to introduce beginning algebra and geometry concepts as fits the case. The task of determining specific standards would also be facilitated by having information such as that provided in table 4.1.

Figure 4.2 Course Requirements for Arithmetic/Mathematics: Grades K–8 (Entry math concepts only)

Key to Checklist

	K	1	2	3	4	5	6	7	8
A. Pre-Number Concepts (math readiness)									
1. Attribute recognition (color, shape, size)	I	M	R	R	R	R	R	R	R
2. Matching	I	M	R	R	R	R	R	R	R
3. Sorting	I	M	R	R	R	R	R	R	R
4. Position (up, down, over, etc.)	I	M	R	R	R	R	R	R	R
5. Quantity (comparisons)	I	M	R	R	R	R	R	R	R
6. Patterns	I	M	R	R	R	R	R	R	R
7. Ordering	I	M	R	R	R	R	R	R	R
B. Counting									
1. By 1 to 100	I	M	R	R	R	R	R	R	R
2. Quantifying	I	M	R	R	R	R	R	R	R

3. Skip counting by fives and tens   I R R R R R R R
4. Skip counting by twos   I R R R R R R R

C. Reading and Writing Whole Numbers

1. Recognize and write 0–9   I R R R R R R R
2. Recognize and write 10–99   M M R R R R R R
3. Recognize and write < 1000   I I I M R R R R
4. Recognize and write < million   I M R R R R
5. Recognize and write < billion   I I R R R R

D. Identifying Fractional Parts

1. Recognize and write proper fractions   I I I M R R R R
2. Recognize and write mixed fractions   I I I M R R R
3. Recognize and write improper fractions   I I M R R R
4. Recognize and write decimals   I I I M R R
5. Decimal/fraction/percent conversion   I I M

E. Place Value—Whole Numbers

1. Two place   I M R R R R R R
2. Three place   I I M R R R R R
3. Commas (thousands, millions, etc.)   I I I M R R R R
4. Expanded notation   I M R R R R R
5. Rounding   I I I I M R R
6. Estimating   I I I I I

F. Order Relationships

1. Ordinal Numbers (1st, 2nd, 3rd)   I I M R R R R R R
2. Number Sentences   I I I I I I I I

G. Place Value—Decimal Numbers

1. Rounding   I I I
2. Estimating   I I I

H. Inequalities

1. Whole numbers   R R M R R R R R
2. Fractions   I I I M R R
3. Decimals   I I M R

I—Initial Instruction
M—Mastery of Introduced Area
R—Reinforcement of Introduced Area

LEARNERS WITH SPECIAL NEEDS

One of education's most impressive accomplishments has been that of providing for learners with special needs. Before 1960, few school districts nationally had extensive programs for students with disabilities. Consider the list of student disabilities that school personnel are serving today. It has been reported that before the enactment of the Education for All Handicapped Children Act (EAHCA) in 1975, only 20 percent of children with disabilities were being educated by public schools in the United States (Norton et al., 2012).

Among the twenty-two disabilities that the majority of school districts are serving today are physical disabilities, bipolar disorder, mental retardation, dyslexia, homelessness, attention deficit disorder, serious emotional disturbances, deaf and hearing impairment, autism, speech and language impairments, Asperger's syndrome, and others. Among the many services that the local school is providing are evaluation and referral services, occupational therapy, psychological services, social work services, home schooling, medical services for diagnostic purposes, rehabilitation services, parental counseling and training services, and others.

Developments in the area of special needs education have brought new and challenging responsibilities for school principals and teachers; new knowledge and skills are required. Reportedly, a school principal spends approximately one-third of his or her time on special needs program activities.

"In addition, principals need to be concerned with all the administrative responsibilities associated with special education, such as staff development, counseling services, home and hospital education services, school health services, parent counseling and training, child-find systems, student rights legislation, and other related activities (Norton et al., 2012). A majority of school principals in one study reported that they were not adequately prepared to meet the requirements of this work.

Special education teachers are among the most "sought after" teacher personnel. Unfortunately, individuals that are certified and highly qualified to do this work can find a much higher salary in occupations outside education. Salaries for administrators, teachers, and specialists in areas such as human disabilities must become a high priority for educational progress in America. It is far past the time that America has to talk about this problem; it is time to do something about it.

A recent article in the *Arizona Republic* (Hansen, 2016) set forth some encouragement for improving educational financial support. The headline reads, "CEOs See Schools as a Key Weakness." The survey of four hundred business executives reported that collectively survey participants didn't see taxes or regulations among their biggest problems. Rather, nearly 75 percent of the executives saw improving K–12 education as the most important task for local governments and 56 percent saw boosting K–12 funding as Arizona's biggest job. This "attitude" certainly is a great improvement over the often heard statement, "Just giving schools more money won't improve education." We submit that if the states want better education, they must pay for it.

PROFESSIONAL ADMINISTRATIVE STANDARDS FOR EDUCATIONAL SUPERVISORS

We submit that little of the foregoing learning concepts is planned, organized, and implemented without the leadership of the school principal, assistant principal, and cooperating supervisors. It is beyond the scope of this book to detail the function of the school principal and assistant principal but we recommend four special resources for further reading. The book *The Principal as a Learning-Leader: Motivating Students by Emphasizing Achievement* (Norton & Kelly, 2012) is an administrator's guide to improving student learning, showing practitioners how to focus on individual academic performance of each and every student and to work with the staff and community to develop learning culture that supports student success. *The Principal as Student Advocate* (Norton et al., 2012) focuses on the endeavor to provide school leaders with tools and techniques that enable them to build a school culture that focuses on student advocacy.

Another book, *Competency-Based Leadership* (Norton, 2013), contends that the school principal is the key to an effective academic program and the high academic performance of students in the school. The stated goals of the school cannot be accomplished without the leadership of the person in the principal's office. New and more challenging roles of the school's assistant principal are detailed in the book *The Assistant Principal's Guide: New Strategies for New Responsibilities* (Norton, 2015). It underscores the fact that current programs of preparation for assistant principals fall short of meeting contemporary needs. With the advent of demands for improved academic performance on the part of all students and the accompanying demands for accountability, new leadership skills and competencies have emerged for school assistant principals. This book serves as an initial guide for meeting these new challenges.

KEY IDEAS AND RECOMMENDATIONS

- Standards-based education does present opportunities to improve programs for student learning. Their focus on the student and his or her continuous improvement is to be commended. Nevertheless, top-down,

mandated curricula and specification for teaching methods by federal or state agencies inhibits the ability of creative local school personnel.
- The concepts of purpose, vision, mission, and standards loom significant in the efforts of school leaders to provide effective school programs for children and youth. Those institutions presently having the responsibility of preparing educational supervisors must give more attention to the matter of learning theories and how practice in this area can be improved.
- Empirical evidence makes it clear that the local school community is in the best position to diagnose the needs and interests of student learners in their schools. Nevertheless, what we do know about learning styles, intelligences, and human motivation is overlooked by professionals in the classroom. It is essential that teacher personnel become more knowledgeable and skilled in the area of human learning.
- The contemporary thinking that "every child succeeds" must be actively pursued. Student retention remains a flawed practice within many national school districts. Educators need to become knowledgeable of the volumes of research that are now available regarding the flawed practice of flunking students in grade.
- The contemporary efforts to implement standards-based report cards for student learning are a step forward. Reporting student performance to parents should be beneficial to parents in their efforts to support their student's academic improvement.
- Professional educational personnel need to become proactive in the effort to retain the local control of education. Although the federal government does have a role in expressing its concerns for improved education, the various states should be responsible for setting the general purposes and aims of education in America, and local school boards and their professional staff should be given the control of planning, implementing, and improving educational experiences of children and youth.

Discussion

1. Assume the role of a school principal at Wymore Middle School who has been asked to present their views on standards-based education at a regular meeting of the school board. Set forth the key points that you will emphasize at the board meeting. What recommendations, for example, will you plan to present?
2. The state education office sent a directive to the school board and administration of your school district. One underlined statement in the directive stated, "Social promotion is discouraged. Students advance or are retained based on their actual learning achievements instead of on their age, their friends' achievement, or tradition." How would you explain or address this statement with your school's faculty? At the

same time, one of your teachers asks the question, "What does the new federal legislation mean in their newest law regarding 'success for all students'?"
3. Consider the proposition, "Education standards for students in public schools should be established by the local school board in cooperation with the administrative and professional staff of the school district." Assume a pro or con position for a debate of this proposition and draft the key points for the argument that you will present.
4. Consider the information in the chapter that focused on educational mandates. If indeed decisions concerning educational standards for student performance were "delegated" to local school districts rather than mandated by state or federal agencies, do you believe that school leaders at the local school level are prepared to accomplish this major task? Why or why not?
5. School purposes were viewed as being of great importance for determining school programs and supervision practices. To what extent, in your opinion, has the concept of purpose, vision, and mission been adopted and practiced in schools within your school district or a district in which you are most familiar? Or is the concept primarily a stagnant statement on a plaque on the school's wall?

CASE STUDY

Case 4.1: Principal Rosales, Your Help Is Needed!

Memo
To: Anna Rosales, Principal
From: Verna Petrov, Grade 3 teacher

I don't want to sound biased, but it seems to me when I have twenty-three children from residents in our district and I get one or two transients who can hardly speak English, it is unfair to expect me to take care of my other students when the other two are so far behind with their knowledge and skills.

I am not asking for more in-service sessions but I need help working with limited ability students and getting them up to grade level. What could you suggest I or we do? The assessments that I have completed indicate that one of the students in the class is actually reading at the second-grade level, and of course his English is on a lower academic level than that.

Discussion

Assume the role of principal Rosales and draft your response to Verna Petrov or write a response that expresses what you would relate to her during a personal conference. Keep in mind the various strategies of standards-based education reported in this chapter.

1. What has been your experience with standards-based report cards? What suggestions might you have for improving this reporting method? How might parents be better informed regarding the standards-based report card system?

    Your school adopted the vision statement, "Failure is no option." List all of the benefits that this statement suggests. Then list what each staff member and the school principal must do to achieve the ends suggested by the statement.

Case 4.2: The Final and Fatal Test

The State Board of Education of Lafayette had been considering the matter of student achievement in grades K–12 for several months. An annual state-mandated Academic Achievement Test (ACT) had been in force for three years. Results of the testing scores were reported for each school in relation to reading, mathematics, social studies, and science for grades 4 to 6 and for grades 7 to 12 at the middle and secondary grades. A school was ranked according to three performance classifications: High Performance, Satisfactory Performance, or Unsatisfactory Performance.

The school principals of underperforming schools were placed on what was viewed as "probation" and after two years of unsatisfactory performance commonly were removed from an administrative position. As one board member commented, "It's time to get tough on student achievement." Nevertheless, no such actions seemed to make a positive difference in student achievement.

Discussions of the student achievement problem set forth many and varied reasons for the dilemma, including student apathy, non-support on the part of parents, unsatisfactory learning leadership on the part of school principals, and others related to the school's curricular offerings.

Many discussions centered on the topics of student differences including the changes in maturity levels of students over their school years.

"Well, if that's the case," stated the president of the school district's school board, "I recommend that we give students the benefit of the doubt and let them show us that they can become competent academically by the end of their senior year. However, besides the usual subjects being tested, I want to recommend that we add a civics section on the final examination.

And, once more, if students don't pass this final exam, no school graduation diploma will be given to them!"

On a vote of 5 to 2, the board president's recommendation was voted into the school district's policy contingent on an opportunity for the school administration to report on its support of the policy.

The school district's administrators' association met to discuss the matter and to select a person to report to the school board on its recommendation and support.

Discussion

(Note: The foregoing case is "fictitious" in regard to the school district and specificity of information. However, the case to some extent parallels the actions of one state at the time of this writing.)

1. Assume the role of a school principal of the Lafayette school district. You have an opportunity to take a stand on the matter at hand. Give serious thought to the matter as set forth in the case, and write your views concerning the matter at hand. Will you recommend the adoption of the school board's pending policy? Why or why not? Set forth the *specific* reasons for your response. That is, avoid such responses as "It all depends" or "I'll just wait and see what the group's consensus might be."
2. To what extent does the question of academic standards come into play in the case?
3. What other concepts set forth in this chapter might serve you in stating your position on the final testing matter?

REFERENCES

Abbott, S. (2014, August 26). *Hidden curriculum.* The glossary of education reform. Retrieved from http://edglossary.org/hidden-curriculum.

Hansen, R. J. (2016, February 17). CEOs see schools as a key weakness. *Arizona Republic,* p. 1A.

Leger, R. (2015, September 3). Real test of education comes many years later. *Arizona Republic,* p. 10A.

Norton, M. S. (2013). *Competency-based leadership: A guide for high performance in the role of the school principal.* Lanham, MD: Rowman & Littlefield.

Norton, M. S. (2015). *The assistant principal's guide: New strategies for new responsibilities.* New York, NY: Routledge.

Norton, M. S., & Kelly, L. K. (2012). *The principal as a learning-leader: Motivating students by emphasizing achievement.* Lanham, MD: Rowman & Littlefield.

Norton, M. S., Kelly, L. K., & Battle, A. R. (2012). *The principal as student advocate: A guide for doing what's best for all students.* Larchmont, NY: Eye on Education.

Sciffiny, P. L. (2008). Seven reasons for standards-based grading. *Educational Leadership, 66*(8), 70–74. Alexandria, VA: ASCD. Retrieved from http://www.ascd.org/publications/educational_leadership/oct08/vol66/num02/Seven_Reasons_for_Standards-Based_

Grading.aspx
Wikipedia. (2016). *Standards of learning.* Retrieved from https://en.wikpedia.org/wiki/Standards_of_learning.

Chapter 5

The School's Curriculum: Local, State, or Federal?

Primary chapter goal: To illustrate the varying concepts of educational curriculum and support the view that teaching and learning and meeting the best interests and needs of students should be a local function.

PART OF THE PUZZLE

A curriculum is a compilation of study materials that are used in all grade levels, classroom and homework assignments, and a set of teacher guides. It could also include a list of prescribed methodology and guidelines of teaching some material for parents. It is generally determined by an external body. However, there are some cases in which it may be developed by the schools and teachers themselves (How to Evaluate Curriculum, 2015).

Only specialists should work on the curriculum (Snedden & Warner, 1927). Many individuals should participate in curriculum planning and development. The full-time job of the school staff is to *deliver* curriculum, not to develop it (Jobrack, 2011). Curriculum builders must include the psychologists, the sociologists, the philosophers, and the teacher, and the work should be done cooperatively (Counts, 1927).

The State Board of Education will assume the role and responsibility for systemwide planning and policy formulation for all public education in the state. We must not continue subject matter or practices that are not justified by social need or that are psychologically wrong (Cox, 1929). The emphasis is less on knowledge and definite skills that all pupils shall get from the curriculum and much more on what *they shall want to know, to do, and to be* (Cox, 1929). Those experiences (curriculum) should be organized into what the teachers believe to be the most effective type of curriculum planning (Chisholm, 1953).

The foregoing examples represent the "problems" of recommending models and suggesting procedures for planning and developing educational curriculum for local schools. Is there any way that the current differences of opinion regarding curriculum decision making can be reconciled? Probably not. However, a synthesis of the literature would support the involvement of the local school district and its teachers in decisions regarding what students should know and be able to do. This chapter centers on the leadership required by school principals and teachers in the planning, organizing, and implementing of curricular studies for children and youth at the local school level. Several models for establishing subject curricular coverage over several grades and related subjects are presented as well.

Today there are great differences among the citizenry as to who should determine what children and youth should know and be able to do and even how such information should be presented. The No Child Left Behind legislation resulted in giving much federal control over public school curriculum. In 2016, however, U.S. Congress passed legislation, the Every Student Succeeds Act, that tends to lessen federal control of education and give back more control to the states and its people. The future of this legislature is yet to be seen. At the time of this writing, Republicans and Democrats were contesting for the presidency and some were standing on election promises to "veto" the Common Core mandates presently in practice.

It is common to hear school principals voice their disenchantment with the Common Core. School administrators and teachers report that the over-intensity of curricular mandates, high-stakes testing, and requirements of instructional methodology inhibit their creative abilities; they feel left out of the decision-making activities of curriculum development within their own school community.

CURRICULUM COMPARISONS: TRADITIONAL CURRICULUM VERSUS STANDARDS-BASED CURRICULUM

Pattison and Berkas (2000) set forth their views of a traditional curriculum approach and a standards-based curriculum process:

> Traditionally, the school curriculum provides a plan of instruction that indicates structured learning experiences and outcomes for students. It specifies the details of student learning, instructional strategies, the teachers' roles, and the context in which teaching and learning take place. More recently, however, the standards movement, research on teaching and learning, and research on characteristics of successful schools have broadened the scope of curriculum

to include everything that affects what happens in the classroom and consequently affects student learning. (p. 5)

The Montana Office of Public Instruction (2016) made an attempt to illustrate the differences between a traditional curriculum approach and a standards-based approach as shown in table 5.1.

We are of the opinion that the traditional curriculum approach is slighted to some extent in Montana's comparative statement. Empirical evidence for the traditional curriculum approach would not commonly begin with a curriculum binder, but rather begin with a representative committee of school district teachers and administrators with the services of a district office coordinator. Initial planning sessions would include input by personnel of the state's education office. The reference to the textbook would have to be extended to the considerations of supplementary instructional resources, including basic, supplementary, and enrichment instructional aides. In addition, ongoing quizzes, unit tests, and final tests are common components of traditional curriculum approaches. Perhaps the major difference between the two curriculum approaches rests in the ways in which the specific standards for classroom teaching are derived.

In addition, historically, traditional curriculum approaches have included vocational/career education as well. A truer picture of the traditional approach would include a direct reference to teacher involvement at the "entry stage" and a more informational statement about external curriculum control. More detailed information concerning curriculum development is presented in the following sections of this chapter.

PROCEDURES FOR CURRICULUM DEVELOPMENT IN THE PUBLIC SCHOOL

Curriculum development commonly follows several specific procedures: diagnosis of student needs (curricular needs assessment); formulation of goals and objectives; curricular fields and courses of study; recommended organization of course content; suggestions for learning experiences and enrich-

Table 5.1

Traditional Curriculum Approach	Standards-Based Curriculum Process
Curriculum Binder	Curriculum>Instruction>Assessment System
Scope and Sequence	Learning Progressions
Textbook	Resources
An Event	Continuous Process
Test at the End	Comprehensive Assessment System

ment experiences; organization of learning experiences (i.e., grade levels and course sequences, evaluation and assessment of learning achievement, and periodic evaluation and assessment of curricular results). In any case, the planning, development, and implementation of curriculum must give paramount attention to societal needs and values, learners' interests and needs, foundational theories and knowledge of learning, school community expectations, and the utilization of organized knowledge.

MODEL FOR CURRICULUM DEVELOPMENT

The following model for curriculum development provides a guide for curriculum committee procedures. Step one is the development of the statement of philosophy and aims for the subject field at a specific grade level such as elementary, middle school, or high school.

Statement of Philosophy and Aims

The curriculum committee develops a statement that expresses its beliefs about education relative to purposes, the nature of learning, nature of the learners, and school community characteristics.

Specific Aims and Purposes

Educational aims and purposes are extensions of a statement of philosophy that reveals the school district's educational mission. The mission sets forth what it is that the school or school district is working to achieve. Historically, national commissions or committees set forth statements regarding the aims and purposes of education in America. For example, more than seventy years ago the Educational Policies Commission (1938) set forth four major objectives that served to guide education in America for many years: the objectives of self-realization, the objectives of human relationships, the objectives of economic efficiency, and the objectives of civic responsibility. These early objectives would be appropriate in many ways for contemporary schools, but specific objectives related to student learning would be a necessary addition.

EXAMPLES OF PHILOSOPHICAL STATEMENTS AS RELATED TO A SCHOOL DISTRICT'S MISSION

- We believe it is the responsibility of the Wymore School District to provide an educational program that will aid children and youth of the community to grow physically, morally, intellectually, and emotionally, so that they may live happily as children and adult citizens of a democracy,

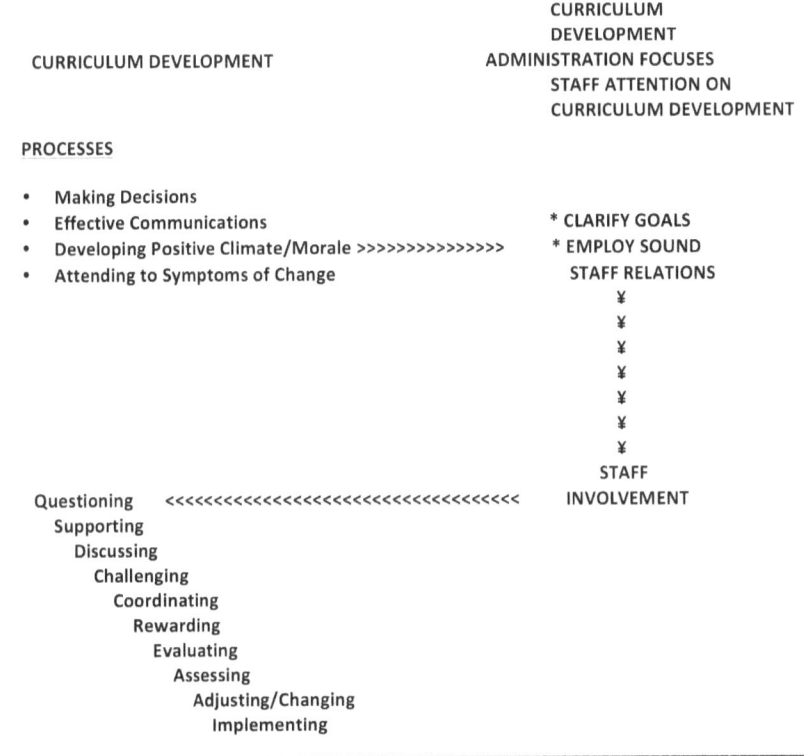

Figure 5.1 Affective Dimensions of Curriculum Development

realizing the most complete life possible within the limits of their individual needs, interests, and abilities.
- We believe that in our democratic society, an opportunity for the development and mastery of fundamental attitudes, habits, and skills must be offered to all learners according to their individual interests, needs, and abilities.
- We believe in the individual worth and dignity of each student. We must provide the ways and means for the individual student to discover and develop his or her abilities and personality that will result in a positive sense of self-esteem and worthy life pursuits in a democratic society.
- We believe that the educational program in the Wymore School District gives each student an understanding, appreciation, and personal involvement in America's democratic society; gives each student the knowledge and skills required by a nation that supports a free enterprise system; and, in the words of President Abraham Lincoln, gives each and every student

an education and the opportunity for a fair chance and unfettered start in the race of life.

STATEMENT OF CURRICULUM GOALS

Goals are precise delineations of the ideals and beliefs expressed in the statement of philosophy or mission. In a specific sense, goals are the applications of the aims expressed in the mission of the school district. What knowledge and skills are expected of the learners as they encounter the curriculum of the school? One of the early statements of educational goals was set forth by the Educational Policies Commission (1938). For example, four of the commission's ten goals were as follows: All youth need to develop salable skills (needed for a successful life), all youth need to develop and maintain good health and physical fitness, all youth need to understand the rights and duties of the citizen in a democratic society, and all youth need to understand the methods of science and other subject areas.

What additional goals would you recommend for your school district? Such goals might include education for international cooperation and peace, education for economic living, education for family living, education for social living, education for rich recreational living, education for communication and learning skills, and others. Goals serve a variety of important educational needs such as serving to establish meaningful standards for student achievement.

GOAL STATEMENTS AND RELATED EDUCATIONAL OBJECTIVES

Consider the goal of communication and learning skills. This goal might be expressed as follows:

> Students shall acquire to the extent of their individual, physical, mental, and emotional capacities a mastery of the basic skills required in maintaining and expressing ideas through the effective use of words, numerals, and other symbols.

Accompanying objectives might be:

> Students shall achieve a working knowledge of reading, writing, and speaking accompanied by gradual development and use of skills in the logical processes of search, analysis, evaluation, and problem solving in critical thinking and in the use of symbolism.

Curriculum objectives ultimately must be developed and accepted at two levels: systemwide cutting across disciplines and grade levels and within a particular discipline or grade level. The statement of objectives should focus on what the learner does or is expected to do as opposed to what the school does. Effectively defined curriculum objectives state what the learner is to achieve, under what conditions he or she must demonstrate the behavior, and the level of performance the student must attain. Note that there is a general distinction between curriculum objectives and instructional objectives. Curriculum objectives are concerned with groups of students and instructional objectives are concerned with individual students in a class or subject.

Let's consider a few examples of curriculum objectives:

Objective 1—To improve the academic performance of high school students.

Indicators of achievement: The number of students scoring above 550 of 800 in either the verbal or math portions of the Scholastic Aptitude Test (SAT) and above 24 on the American College Test (ACT) will increase by 5 percent in 2017 and again by 5 percent in 2018.

Objective 2—To decrease the dropout rates of students in the school by 10 percent within the next two years.

Objective 3—To increase the reading scores of elementary school students by 20 percent within the next two years.

Objective 4—To increase the number of students participating in the school's honor program by 5 percent by the next school year.

THE PLANNING AND DEVELOPMENT OF LOCAL SCHOOL SYSTEM CURRICULUM GUIDES

A curriculum guide is a general plan for a particular sequence of grade levels for a subject field such as reading, mathematics, social studies, or science. Curriculum guides commonly are developed for the purpose of recommending a systematic program of studies for a subject or program of studies within the elementary, middle school, or high school grades. It enables the school district to maintain a viable program of studies as students move through the school as a system.

As pointed out by the Connecticut State Department of Education (2016), "A curriculum guide is a document that delineates the philosophy, goals, objectives, learning experiences, instructional resources and assessments that comprise a specific educational program. . . . It represents an articulation of what students should know and be able to do and supports teachers in knowing how to achieve these goals" (p. 1).

A curriculum guide commonly includes the following components:

a. Introduction of purposes, goals, and objectives: The guide opens with reference to the school district's curriculum goals and objectives within a particular field of study or grade level.
b. Instructional goals: The goal in mathematics might state that students should complete the mathematics sequence with competence in mathematics that will enable them to function in their daily personal transactions.
c. Instructional objectives: An objective might state that the completion of the mathematics sequence for six graders will result in having 90 percent of them scoring a grade of 65 percent or better on the terminal math test developed by local teachers or as set forth by the state.
d. Sequence of topics: In this section, the intended topical content or units to be included in a course of study or grade are presented in logical sequence. The scope of the content to be included for the course or grade is outlined for a specific period of time of instruction (e.g., year or semester). In most instances, one should be able to trace the production of curriculum from the curriculum guide to a resource unit, to a teaching/learning unit, and to a specific lesson plan.
e. Learning activities and strategies: This section of the guide sets forth suggested instructional strategies and activities based on the instructional objectives, the content of the unit, and the interests and needs of the learners. We emphasize the fact that such instructional strategies are suggested as opposed to required. We keep in mind that teacher turnover brings new teachers to the school district every year; many are first-year teachers. Learning activities include a wide variety of provisions, methods, and extensions for the teacher's consideration. Best practices set forth by basic and empirical research as well as those suggested by local teachers are appropriate for this section.
f. Evaluation plan: In today's schools, the student evaluation and assessment requirements tend to be mandated by state agencies. We recommend a local procedure for evaluating the school's curriculum. Both formal and informal measures are recommended for assessment purposes, including oral and written quizzes, observation, norm-referenced tests and criterion-referenced tests, self-assessment strategies, portfolios, work samples, and standardized tests that fit the case. Nevertheless, less time for testing and more time for learning is our recommendation. The following section focuses on the purposes, procedures, evaluative criteria, unmet needs, and designing and implementing a follow-up process.

The formulation of such a school or school district curriculum guide should not be viewed as the culmination of the curriculum development process, but rather as an essential step in the process of ongoing curricular development and implementation. (Connecticut State Department of Education, 2016, p. 1)

CURRICULUM MAPPING AND ITS VALUES

Even though the school and school district have developed curriculum for guidance on what students are to know and be able to do, the need is to know what is actually being taught in the classroom. *Curriculum mapping* is an analysis of what a teacher has actually taught and the amount of time he or she has spent on tasks: an analysis of the real curriculum. Curriculum mapping tells you the level of repetition that exists or does not exist in the instruction, how teachers spend time on task, and information about the real curriculum to make adjustments in such things as the testing program.

Curriculum mapping, then, describes the curriculum as it currently exists. Eventually, the school staff is able to make the written curriculum and the actual curriculum more congruent. In addition, curriculum mapping can reveal variations in topics taught and time spent among teachers of all sections of the same grade level or subject. The mapping strategy differs from the teacher's actual lesson plan. A lesson plan is what the teacher plans to do in the future. Curriculum mapping is what the teacher is doing or has done in the past. A major value of curriculum mapping is that it provides information for the curriculum committee or the curriculum coordinator regarding how much time teachers are spending on each major subject or subject area.

CURRICULUM NEEDS ASSESSMENT

A curriculum needs assessment seeks to determine whether stated goals and objectives have been met. In view of the school's stated objectives of the school, which objectives are not being achieved? Thus, it serves as a tool to underscore the gaps between current performance results and desired academic results. Questions such as the following should be asked: "Which needs show important gaps and should be ones of highest priority for remediation?"

There are five major steps in the assessment process. (1) Objectives serve as the starting point for a needs assessment. Objectives commonly are ranked according to importance or priority. (2) Assessment data commonly include teachers' records, standardized test results, student portfolios or work completed and graded, guidance records, mapping results, and teacher evaluations. This step looms important in regard to the school's performance liabilities. (3) Evaluative criteria are determined by the curriculum committee. Evaluative criteria must be determined. Committee members' judgments concerning the extent to which curricular objectives have been met loom important. Questions such as the following are posed: "Are the curricular/instructional objectives in place valid?" "Which of the curricular needs set forth have not been met?" "Are the present curricular objectives valid?" (4) The criteria for ranking the importance/priority of unmet needs are determined. "How are the judgments of committee members and others within the school faculty to be involved in the valuing of unmet needs?" (5) The follow-up process: "How will the recommendations of the curriculum committee be processed?"

The following presents a position description for a curriculum coordinator. The role of curriculum coordinator more commonly is one within the local school although it might be a part-time position in some schools with smaller student populations. In any case, the position description is illustrative rather than being a specific model that meets every school's organizational needs.

POSITION DESCRIPTION FOR A CURRICULUM COORDINATOR

Title: Curriculum Coordinator
Position Qualifications:

1. Valid teacher's certification with a master's degree in curriculum and supervision.
2. A minimum of three years of teaching experience at the grade levels of the assignment.
3. Record of professional experience in school curriculum development activities, workshops, and other related curriculum program experiences.

Reports to: Building principal(s)
Supervises: Assists school principal(s) in the planning, development, implementation, and assessment of curriculum programs for the grade levels assigned.
Position Goal: To achieve and maintain standards of excellence in the program areas assigned so that each student may derive the greatest academic and personal benefits from the school's learning experiences.
Performance Responsibilities:

1. Plans, organizes, and presides over departmental instructional meetings, workshops, and other curricular sessions for assigned areas of the school's program.

2. Promotes and holds pre-service and in-service meetings in assigned curricular areas.
3. Prepares opportunities for teachers to observe teaching demonstrations by highly qualified teachers within the school system.
4. Works directly with school principals, assistant principals, and department heads in the planning and implementation of curricular development.
5. Prepares special reports concerning curricular evaluations and assessment of program results.
6. Serves as the chair of curriculum revision studies for subject areas within the school and the selection of appropriate instructional materials for the subject areas being examined.
7. Sets forth a communication system for reporting and discussing research studies and empirical results of experimental programs.
8. Conducts analyses of instructional programs and materials and works to foster courses that are designed to set forth the scope and sequence of subjects for effective learning results.
9. Serves as a resource leader for curriculum experimentation, curriculum evaluations and assessments, and in-service workshops and learning centers.
10. Cooperates with the school principals, teachers, librarian, and media personnel in establishing and maintaining a professional library for teachers and administrators and the use of effective technology in the classroom.
11. Provides leadership in the development of a relevant program of instruction for the grade levels related to the position assignment and works cooperatively with other curriculum coordinators within the K–12 school system to ensure a correlated and integrated school system program of studies.

Terms of Employment: Twelve (12) months with appropriate vacation time and salary as approved by the Board of Education.

Position Evaluation: Performance of the position is evaluated annually in accordance with provisions set forth in policy on the evaluation of administrative personnel. Each curriculum coordinator will establish a set of position goals and objectives annually with his or her respective supervisor.

A STANDARDS-BASED HIGH SCHOOL CURRICULUM

In the previous chapter, several examples of standards-based curricular programs and report cards were discussed. In the following section a comprehensive example of a school district's standards-based curriculum is set forth. This example, however, is quite different from those program samples discussed previously. This high school curriculum is based on Common Core requirements. It is important to note that the curricular standards set forth in Figure 5.2A are ones that have been selected by the school district's professional staff from the many core standards recommended by the state. Although the standards are those chosen from the state's core, the standards shown in Figure 5.2A depict those selected by teachers of grades 6 through 12 as being appropriate for the school's curricular program for reading, writing, speaking and listening, and language.

Note in Figure 5.2A that all of the recommended standards were selected. The selected standards(s) are those standards given priority by the school district. Changes are likely to be implemented as follow-up evaluations and assessments of program results are known.

Figure 5.2B is an example of career ready standards for mathematics courses. The "S" notation indicates the selected standards for one school district's program. It is presented as an illustration only and is not to be considered as exemplary or applicable for every school district's math program.

THE CO-CURRICULUM: A CONSTRUCTIVE PART OF A STUDENT'S EDUCATION

Co-curricular activities, although perceived as being dispensable, are a constructive part of a student's education. Co-curricular activities are practical and recreational experiences that commonly take place outside of regular course work, carry no credit, serve educational purposes, and relate to the goals and objectives of the school's program.

Co-curricular activities include school sports, clubs, assembly programs, homeroom activities, field trips, camping, intramural sports activities, recreational development, and more recently a religious discussion group activity. In a 1990 law case, *Westside Community Schools v. Mergens*, 496 U.S. 226, a senior high school student asked permission to initiate an after-school Christian club. The high school had several student clubs associated with the school and U.S. Congress had recently passed the Equal Access Act, which allowed schools to permit religious clubs if other student interest clubs were in existence. The Supreme Court ruled in favor of the high school student and stated that allowing students to meet on campus after school to discuss religion did not amount to state sponsorship of religion.

Co-curricular activities serve several important purposes. Effective co-curriculum programs serve to meet the special interests of students or to develop new interests. Many such activities supplement and enrich the

		6	7	8	9	10	11	12
Range of Writing	Routine writing over extended and shorter time frames	S	S	S	S	S	S	S
Comprehension & Collaboration	Conversations and collaboration with diverse groups	S	S	S	S	S	S	S
	Evaluation of information in different formats	S	S	S	S	S	S	S
	Speaker's point of view	S	S	S	S	S	S	S
Presentation of Knowledge & Ideas	Presentations	S	S	S	S	S	S	S
	Strategic use of media & tools	S	S	S	S	S	S	S
	Speeches for a variety of contexts and tasks	S	S	S	S	S	S	S
Conventions of Standard English	Commands of conventions in writing and speaking	S	S	S	S	S	S	S
	Capitalization, punctuation, and spelling in writing	S	S	S	S	S	S	S
Knowledge of Language	Language functions in different contexts, meaning, style, and comprehension	S	S	S	S	S	S	S
Vocabulary Acquisition and Use	Context clues and word parts	S	S	S	S	S	S	S
	Figurative language, word relationships, nuances	S	S	S	S	S	S	S
	Academic and domain-specific words independently	S	S	S	S	S	S	S

Figure 5.2A School Standards for Grades 6 to 12 English Language Arts

school's organized classroom experiences. Such programs supplement educational objectives such as worthy use of leisure time, social relationships, psychomotor skills, physical development, and others. Some activities serve to foster and enrich school spirit and morale, develop teamwork, and reveal students' interests in a different context.

In regard to scheduling, co-curricular activities must be an actual part of the school's schedule and supervised by a qualified teacher or other qualified individual. Such activities must extend the school day and must not interrupt the ongoing school curriculum program. Teachers as sponsors of co-curricular activities must be given credit as part of their teaching assignment and workload. In our view, such sponsorship assignments should be compensated commensurately above the teacher's regular teacher load.

Conceptual Category	Domain	Algebra 1-2	Geometry 1-2	Algebra Apps	Algebra 3-4	Pre-Calculus	College Math	College Alg.	Probability
Real Number System	S		S	S				S	
Quantities	S		S	S	S		S	S	
Complex Numbers			S	S		S			S
Vector Quantities					S		S		
Structure in Expressions	S		S		S		S		S
Polynomials & Rational Expressions	S	S		S		S		S	
Creating Expressions	S	S		S		S		S	
Creating Equations	S	S		S		S		S	
Equations & Inequalities	S		S		S		S	S	S
Interpreting Functions	S	S		S		S		S	S
Building Functions	S	S		S		S		S	S
Linear, Quadratic, & Exponential Models	S	S		S		S		S	S
Trigonometric Functions			S		S		S		

Figure 5.2B School Standards for Grades 6 to 12 Mathematics

REVIEW QUIZ

Take a few minutes to complete the following quiz concerning the information set forth thus far in the chapter. If you do not know the answer, do not guess but go on to the next question. The answers to the quiz are given at the end of the quiz. Circle the correct answer for each question.

1. The primary purpose of chapter 5 is to:

    a. Support the implementation of Common Core in school district programs.
    b. Support standards-based school curriculum for all public schools.
    c. Support more local control of school curriculum for all public schools.
    d. Illustrate what a curriculum coordinator should do.

2. One important point set forth in this chapter was to:

    a. Point out the differences of opinion regarding what and how the school's curriculum should be implemented.

b. Demonstrate the importance of the federal government's involvement in curriculum development.
c. Encourage school principals to adopt the Common Core standards.
d. Set forth a model for a standards-based report card.

3. This chapter underscores the point that:

   a. Traditional- and standards-based curricula really have no differences.
   b. Traditional- and standards-based curricula differ primarily by the role of the federal government in curriculum development.
   c. Standards-based report cards have no place in the reporting practices of effective schools.
   d. None of the above.

4. Local control by the school district and local schools is in the best position to:

   a. Determine what is best for meeting student interests and needs.
   b. Gain the motivation for teachers to be creative in the classroom.
   c. Gain the involvement of teachers in the building of a school district's curriculum program.
   d. Accomplish all of the above.

5. Curriculum mapping is the process of:

   a. Illustrating what should be taught in the classroom.
   b. Illustrating the schedule of lessons for each subject to be taught.
   c. Illustrating what is actually being taught in a subject or curricular field.
   d. Giving each teacher a standard lesson plan for daily classroom lessons.

Quiz Answers

Question 1: The answer is c; the primary purpose of chapter 5 was to support more local control of the school's curriculum for all public schools. We have emphasized the belief that the local school principal and the professional staff are in the best position to determine the individual interests and needs of the children and youth that they serve. It is not that curriculum decisions are the exclusive rights of the local school. Rather, as illustrated by Figure 5.2, the curriculum is developed by the local school in accord with the needs of children and youth and the demands of the society (i.e., the local school community). These two factors cooperate in determining the program of the school. The program of the school, in turn, is the school's curriculum that sets forth what the students are to learn and be able to do along with the related services that the school provides.

Figure 5.2 presents a general procedure for curriculum development from the sources of influence on curriculum provisions to the measurement of outcomes and the assessment of achievement gaps.

Question 2: The answer is a. A variety of internal and external "forces" influences, inhibits, or facilitates the decisions as to the actual curricular program that is established in the local school. One school principal, for example, informed us that a listing of any and all instructional resources being used by a schoolteacher must first be approved by the local school board. With interventions and mandates of state and federal agencies, local curriculum decisions have become problematic.

More than thirty years ago, Christensen (1980) noted that three primary conditions tend to influence the current state of curriculum development. First of all, there is a lack of accurate conceptualization and a consensus on the major constructs of curriculum development. Secondly, there is a lack of leadership among educators with abilities to conceptualize, develop, implement, monitor, and evaluate effective curriculum design. Thirdly, there is a lack of specification and differentiation in the roles of superintendents of schools (including associates and building principals) who must assume leadership roles. We submit that these conditions remain in contemporary practices and are further enhanced by the ongoing controls of federal agencies.

Question 3: The answer is b. We have emphasized the principle that education is a federal concern, state responsibility, and local function. Standards-based curriculum holds promise for improving the education program for children and youth. However, we contend that such mandated standards established by the federal government are contrary to the intent of the U.S. Constitution and result in inhibiting the ability of local schools to determine what actually is in the best interests and needs of students.

Figure 5.4 sets forth Tomlinson's (2016) concept of differentiated instruction. Differentiated instruction has the purpose of giving educators help in understanding the basis of the concept and the tools needed to be confident in meeting the needs of their diverse students' population.

We encourage you to secure a copy of the book *The Principal as a Learning-Leader*. This book focuses on those individuals in schools that are faced with many of the contemporary problems related to such matters as

Curriculum Development

Needs of Children		Demands of Society
	Determine the Program of the School Which Is	
The Curriculum of the School	+	The Services of the School

The Process of Curriculum Development

SOURCES of THE CURRICULUM

Needs of Individual Students
Needs of Society
Society Values
Organized Human Knowledge
Empirical and Basic Research
Education Personnel
Education Committees/Recommendations

STATEMENT OF PURPOSE—VISION & MISSION

School Philosophy
School Vision
School Mission

CURRICULUM DESIGN

Subjects
Goals/Objectives
Rationale, Scope
Performance Objectives
Learning Standards

IMPLEMENTATION

Instructional Strategies
Methods of Instruction
Instructional Resources
System Programming

EVALUATION AND ASSESSMENT

Evaluation of Curriculum
Evaluation Strategies
Testing Outcomes
Personnel Input
Curriculum Gaps
Learning Gaps
Follow-up Program Improvement Strategies

Performance Objectives

Learning Standards

IMPLEMENTATION

Instructional Strategies

Methods of Instruction

Instructional Resources

System Programming

EVALUATION AND ASSESSMENT

Evaluation of Curriculum

Evaluation Strategies

Testing Outcomes

Personnel Input

Curriculum Gaps

Learning Gaps

Follow-up Program Improvement Strategies

Figure 5.3 Curriculum Development

underperforming schools, student dropout rates, low student achievement, and student performance accountability.

It has become troublesome for teachers to be creative in meeting the individual interest and needs of their students because Common Core standards tend to specify not only what is to be taught but also the method that must be implemented. We believe that the teacher should be the one that designs, adapts, and delivers instruction to meet each student's diverse learning strengths and needs by creating opportunities for students to demonstrate their learning according to their learning styles.

Question 4: The answer is a. Perhaps we have sufficiently answered the rationale for this answer in the preceding responses. Both teacher and principals express the opinion that current mandated curricular provisions lead both to their frustration of teaching and to the question as to whether or not they wish to remain as a teacher in the classroom.

Question 5: The answer is c. What a teacher has actually taught and the amount of time he or she spent on tasks are determined by mapping. It is concerned with the real curriculum to adjust subject content, testing, and curriculum guides. What is the level of the teacher's repetition? How much time is spent on task? How does what is being taught match what is written in

DIFFERENTIATION

Is a response to learners' needs

Guided by mindset and general principles of differentiation

Respectful tasks | Quality curriculum | Teaching up | Flexible grouping | Continual assessment | Building community

Teachers can differentiate through

Content | Process | Product | Affect | Learning Environment

According to Students'

Readiness | Interest | Learning Profile

Using Instructional Strategies (such as)

Scaffold Reading | Learning Contracts | Learning Interest Centers | Intelligence Preferences | Others

Figure 5.4 Model for Meeting Individual Student Needs. Source: Carol Tomlinson Ed.D. *Teacher Resources, Differentiated Resources for Diverse Learners*. From the web: http://nshuman.weebly.com/differentiated-instruction-for-diverse-learners (1/6/2016).

the school's curriculum guide? What variations in topics are taught among all teachers of the same section of the same grade or subject area?

KEY IDEAS AND RECOMMENDATIONS

- Historically there has been a wide variation among people, associations, and levels of government concerning the curriculum of public schools: what is to be taught and how it is to be taught to students. Although the U.S. Constitution infers that education is referred to the states and its people, the federal government has assumed considerable control of local school's educational program offerings. The No Child Left Behind legislation, at the time of this writing, was about to be replaced by new legislation, Every Student Succeeds. If this legislation ultimately is approved, reportedly more educational control will be returned to the states and local school districts.
- Traditional curriculum and standards-based curriculum do have commonalities. A major difference between the two is that of the controls set forth by the federal government in programs such as Common Core based on mandated curricular provisions and methods of teaching.

- Local control that gives each state the authority to prescribe the primary purposes of education and leaves the discretion for curriculum development and implementation to the local school district is preferred for several reasons. One reason is that of being able to determine the real needs and interests of the students whom they teach.
- Such strategies as curriculum mapping serve to determine what actually is being taught in the classroom and how it coincides with the official curriculum of the school.
- There are valid procedures for school leaders to follow in planning, organizing, developing, implementing, evaluating, and assessing the school's curriculum. Nevertheless, it is questionable whether or not administrator preparation programs are giving high priority to curriculum development.
- Administrator preparation programs necessarily must do much more to instill the required knowledge and skill in curriculum development on the part of aspiring school leaders if local schools are to assume this responsibility.
- The chapter sets forth several examples of standards-based curriculum and standards-based reporting of student progress. These examples are recommended for consideration only. The need is for local schools to work with the professional staff in developing their own standards-based offerings for students and will prove beneficial to all those concerned.

Discussion

1. Give consideration to the extent that you believe you or other professional personnel in your school, or one for which you are most familiar, are prepared to assume leadership for the planning and implementation of the school's curriculum.
2. Assume that you or your school leaders were given a greater degree of autonomy for curriculum development in your school. What curricular program and curriculum process changes would you recommend?
3. You have been asked to address the school's Parent Teacher Association on the topic of the curriculum. What three or four major points would you plan to set forth in your remarks? What specific recommendations might you set forth?

CASE STUDY

Case 5.1: Memo to Principal Anna Gomez

To: Principal Anna Gomez
From: Pat Ramirez

Re: Recommendations for future in-service programs

I realize that you took a schoolteacher survey concerning perceived needs in the school but the listing that was set forth by you really did not include my recommendations. None of the listed in-service ideas unfortunately would meet my needs. When we are asked to work with each student at his or her instructional level—when I have twenty-five students with three or four that can hardly speak English—it seems somewhat ludicrous to expect me to take care of the other twenty-one students (who also have varying abilities) and then the other slower learners are so far behind.

As I read the standards for fourth-grade students, each student is expected to meet a specific standard score on the state tests. It's almost like asking each and every student to be able to clear a three-foot high jump by the end of the year. With our current grade report card, I have to assign a grade of F to each of these slow learners, even though they are making some learning progress. With our present curriculum standards and the high-stakes testing, No Child Left Behind doesn't seem even possible.

Perhaps several of our in-service programs could deal with this problem. Thank you.

Discussion

1. Assume the role of Principal Gomez and respond to Ms. Ramirez either in a memo or set forth the points that you would underscore in a personal conference with her. Be specific in your remarks. Your intent should be to help her resolve the problem(s) that she is encountering. For example, what might you be able to discuss with her regarding the traits of slow learners (e.g., slow learners prefer simpler tasks, have shorter attention spans, want to work at their own pace, etc.)? Consider strategies such as finding the slow learner's areas of interest, checking on a student's nutrition and food habits, and so forth.

REFERENCES

Chisholm, L. E. (1953). *The work of the modern high school.* New York, NY: The Macmillan Company.

Christensen, D. D. (1980, December). Curriculum development: A function of design and leadership. *The Executive Review, 1*(3).

Connecticut State Department of Education. (2016, February 19). *Guide to curriculum development: Purposes, practices, procedures.* Bureau of Curriculum and Instruction. Hartford, CT: Author.

Cox, P. W. L. (1929). *The junior high school curriculum.* New York, NY: Charles Scribner's Sons.

Educational Policies Commission. (1938). *The purposes of education in American democracy.* Washington, DC: National Education Association.

Montana Office of Public Instruction. (2016, January 14). Standard-based curriculum. In *Curriculum development guide*. Helena, MT: Author.

Pattison, C., & Berkas, N. (2000). *Critical issue: Integrating standards into the curriculum*. In North Central Mathematics and Science Consortium at North Central Regional Education Laboratory. Retrieved from http://www.ncrel.org.sdrs/areas/issues/content/curriculum/cu300.html

Snedden, D., & Warner, W. (1927). *Reconstruction of industrial arts courses*. New York, NY: Teachers College/Columbia University.

Tomlinson, C. (2016, January 6). Differentiated instruction for diverse learners. *Teacher Resources*. Retrieved from http://www.edutopia.org/blog/differentiated-instruction-strategies-pbl-andrew-miller

Westside Community Schools v. Mergens, 496 U.S. 226 (1990).

Chapter 6

Supervision: Improving Classroom Teaching

Primary chapter goal: To guide the school principal toward becoming an effective instructional program supervisor.

THE STORY OF MERTON

Merton was a first-year social studies teacher at Wymore Middle School. He received grades of satisfactory in most all of his courses during his work on a bachelor of science degree with a major in education. He completed one semester as a practice teacher in a different middle school in the Wymore School District. Again his practice teaching was rated as satisfactory. The principal that supervised Merton's practice teaching wrote on his grade report that "Merton Horning performed satisfactorily and should continue to improve with additional teaching experience."

The Wymore School District's policy stated that nontenured teachers were to be evaluated twice each semester. Merton was assigned four classes of social studies that included American History, Civics, and two classes of State History. Principal Meierhenry performed three walk-through visits to Merton's classroom before the first formal performance observation after the first six weeks of school.

The principal had visited with Merton on two occasions about the need for him to improve his classroom management as well as the need for him to vary his teaching methods for the purpose of engaging his students in the learning process. Although Merton was following the school's curriculum guides in each of his courses, his lecture style of teaching was not holding the attention of his pupils.

The first test results for Merton's students at the end of the first six weeks of classes were quite disappointing. Fifty percent of the students in Merton's American History class failed the final test and test results in his other two courses were much the same. It was obvious to Principal Meierhenry that in-service supervision was needed in Merton's case.

Principal Meierhenry implemented a variety of improvement activities for Merton, including the observation of other highly qualified teachers, mentoring sessions that centered on class preparation and effective lesson planning, the use of technology in the classroom, the videotaping of his teaching performance, clinical supervision procedures, and other activities such as having Merton attend the state social study teachers' conference. It was clear to others that Principal Meierhenry was devoting a lion's share of his supervisory time toward helping Merton improve. Unfortunately, things did not improve. Student and parental complaints increased. Student achievement test scores decreased. By the end of the first semester, it was apparent that changes had to be made in Merton's work assignment.

Thought was given to the fact that continuing the improvement activities for Merton might result in some improvement by the end of the second semester. That is, his present unsatisfactory performance might be brought up to a level of actual mediocrity. But this thought brought the principal and others to the fact that mediocrity would not be satisfactory. In addition, Principal Meierhenry was of the opinion that spending the same amount of time with high-performing teachers would be far more productive.

Merton asked to be released before the start of the second semester. His resignation was accepted.

The point of Merton's story is vested in the matter of spending the majority of time on trying to improve poor teaching. Bringing an unsatisfactory teacher up to the level of mediocrity is troublesome, at best, especially when other teachers' performances could be improved from marginal to satisfactory or from satisfactory to highly qualified. Principal Meierhenry's efforts to help Merton could be viewed as laudatory. In fact, state requirements for teacher dismissal resulting from "incompetence" commonly must be accompanied with evidence that the teacher in question was given instructional support. However, spending the lion's share of a principal's supervisory time to bring a performance to the level of mediocrity must be questioned.

Shouldn't the determination of teaching competency be determined before licensing is granted? Norton (2015a) is of the opinion that the problem of marginal teachers will continue until teacher preparation programs take the necessary step to make certain that prospective teachers have demonstrated the characteristics of high-quality professionals before being licensed. Although on-the-job professional development is needed and is most acceptable, on-the-job preparation is not. As is done in many other professional occupations, requirements such as long-term internships and follow-up experiences in two- to four-year residencies are expected before "final licensing" is granted. For further information concerning the issues and problems of hiring quality teachers, we recommend the following reference: *The Changing Landscape of School Leadership: Recalibrating the School Principalship* (2015).

SNAPSHOT 1: SOAR WITH YOUR STRENGTHS

A principal of an elementary school in Arizona asked for a conference with her master's degree advisor. She reported that she was experiencing personnel problems at her school with unsatisfactory classroom teaching performances, apathy, and a lack of cooperation and morale. The principal had worked diligently in an attempt to improve the glaring weaknesses of individual faculty members without success. She had scheduled in-service activities on several occasions that centered on the identified weaknesses of the several teachers and had implemented mentoring sessions that focused on areas of instructional needs as well. The mood of the principal was such that she expressed the feeling that she was planning to leave the principalship and return to the classroom.

Her advisor, a university professor, had read the book *Soar with Your Strengths* (Clifton & Nelson, 1992). The professor discussed the concepts set forth in the book with the principal and loaned his copy of the book to the principal. The authors emphasized that organizations will realize greater personnel performance by developing and using the strengths of its human assets rather than focusing on their weaknesses. The principal came back to the professor's office a few weeks later to return his book and tell him of the results of her actions with the teachers in her school. She had ceased the attention that was focused on the individual teacher's weaknesses and encouraged them to implement their personal strengths in their lesson plans and classroom instruction. With a big smile on her face, she reported that the positive changes in the school's climate and teachers' performances were nothing more than a miracle.

A supervisor is a person formally designated to interact with faculty personnel to improve the quality of learning for students. Supervision is directly concerned with student learning outcomes, ways to achieve these outcomes, and the assessment and evaluation of learning results. The four major domains of supervision are administrative tasks, instructional improvement tasks, curriculum improvement tasks, and staff development tasks. In this chapter, we give primary attention to administrative, instructional, and staff development tasks because the topic of curriculum was detailed in the previous chapter. Conducting relative research, determining instructional goals and objectives, preparing instructional programs, and developing curriculum program guides are common tasks of curriculum coordinators at the district and local school levels. The central focus of supervision, under any one of its many definitions, must be undergirded by those activities directly related to improvement of teaching and improved curricular provisions that lead to improved student learning.

General supervision includes all activities performed by supervisory personnel and is related but not the same as administration. Commonly, general supervision consists of activities that take place outside the classroom. On the other hand, instructional supervision includes activities related to either general or clinical supervision. Instructional supervision is performed specifically toward the goal of instructional improvement. Clinical supervision includes activities that occur in the classroom, although pre-observation and post-observation conferencing by the teacher and supervisor do take place outside the student-teacher classroom setting.

Instructional supervision is differentiated from such activities as supervising facilities, transportation, the cafeteria, and other maintenance activities. Other instructional tasks commonly include the evaluation and assessment of program standards, coordination of instructional in-service programs, working with administrators and faculty personnel on curriculum guides, mentoring activities and instructional resources selection, and serving as resources people for advising and assisting administrative and staff personnel.

THE MIX OF INSTRUCTIONAL SUPERVISORS

Not only do the position titles of instructional supervisors widely differ, but other conditions such as job authority, primary job functions, position location, immediate supervisors, subject-area assignments, grade jurisdiction, time commitments, and contacts with teacher personnel also differ.

Although it is beyond the scope of this chapter to discuss in detail all of the position differences evidenced in the roles of the instructional supervisor nationally, the following information provides some insights into the mix of instructional supervision nationally:

- Approximately two-thirds of instructional supervisors assume the position from a teaching role. The remaining one-third of the supervisors most commonly were former department or grade-level heads.
- The most common title for people in instructional leadership roles is instructional specialist, although educational personnel serving in this position at the school district office most often have the titles of assistant superintendent or assistant superintendent for instruction. Director of instruction and coordinator of curriculum are other common titles.

- The position of an instructional supervisor is viewed by people in the position as either being a line position or a staff position. In one reported study, the division between the two perspectives was virtually equal. A line position is viewed as being in the *line of authority* within the school system, whereas a staff position is viewed as a service role as opposed to a control position.
- Staff development, curriculum development, classroom observation, program evaluation, articulation of the curriculum, teaching methods/strategies, instructional materials selection, instructional resources consultant, curriculum research development, pupil achievement evaluation, teacher evaluation, and school climate development are among the most common work responsibilities of the instructional supervisor.
- Teachers lead the list of groups with whom supervisors are most frequently in contact. However, frequent contacts with various school administrators are common as well.
- The largest number of instructional supervisors reportedly have a twelve-month contract. Although some contract salaries are tied to the teachers' salary schedule, more commonly salaries are tied to the school district's administrators' salary schedule.
- Keeping up to date reportedly is one of the greatest problems of instructional supervisors. The changing requirements of state and federal mandates tend to be the underlying reason for this contention. However, top-down curricular requirements place local school leaders in the role of carrying out the plans of others as opposed to taking the leadership for identifying curricular needs and taking the leadership for coordinating the efforts of school personnel in implementing and evaluating program results.
- An evaluation of the instructional supervisor's performance is required of all instructional supervisors. However, such an evaluation is completed by a number of different school administrators depending on the location of the instructional supervisor's office and the variances of their immediate supervisor.

Related administrative supervisory tasks commonly include involvement in the hiring of personnel, recommending policies and procedures in the areas of curriculum and supervision, handling instructional resources and supplies, and providing instructional facilities such as teacher centers and professional educational libraries. In addition, thought must be given to the often overlooked matter of teacher load. As noted by Norton (2008), "Staff assignment requires that careful attention be given to teacher load. Without such consideration, inequities in the workload are certain to persist, and personnel who are most qualified to carry out an effective educational program in the school often are so overburdened that their efforts are forced to a level of mediocrity" (p. 168). The topic of teacher load is discussed later in the chapter.

So as an instructional supervisor, the school principal must be knowledgeable and skilled in developing curriculum, organizing for instruction, helping in the hiring of qualified staff, providing suitable learning facilities and materials, arranging for effective staff development, orientating new personnel, relating to the special needs program of the school, initiating an effective public relations program, and evaluating and assessing instruction. He or she must wear the hats of leader, coordinator, and evaluator/assessor. Two important questions must be posed: Are school principals being prepared to take the leadership required for meeting these tasks? Is on-the-job experience sufficient to meet the demands of effective curricular development and instructional improvement?

WHAT DOES AN EFFECTIVE LESSON PLAN LOOK LIKE?

Developing effective lesson plans is among the first priorities of an instructional supervisor for helping a new teacher and others learn the importance of identifying the objectives for student learning, the activities that will be used to achieve the objectives, and the strategies for assessing if and what a student has learned. Milkova (2016) set forth seven steps for preparing a lesson including specific questions that must be addressed in relation to each procedural step in the process.

- Step 1: Outline Learning Objectives—What it is that the teacher wants the students to know and be able to do at the end of the lesson. Examples of questions that must be answered by the teacher include: "What do I want students to learn?" and "What topics are of most importance?"
- Step 2: Develop the Introduction—Establish an engagement set for the lesson. For example, "How best might I introduce the lesson?" "How will I tie the lesson to what they have learned previously?" "How can I engage the students in the learning process at the outset of the lesson?"
- Step 3: Plan the Specific Learning Activities for the Lesson—Just how will the teacher "teach" the topics to be learned? What information will be presented, discussed, and assessed? What methods and/or strategies will be most effective for student learning?
- Step 4: Plan to Check for Understanding—"How will I know if students have learned/understood the information/concepts presented?" "What questions will I ask to check understanding?"
- Step 5: Develop a Conclusion and a Preview—Summarize the main points/knowledge of the lesson. "What will I have students do to illus-

trate that they have understood/learned what was discussed and/or presented?"

Step 6: Create a Realistic Timeline—Estimate the time that each major lesson objective will take and adjust the lesson as needed. Great teachers find that lesson adjustments are common in their classrooms. Be prepared to monitor and adjust your instruction.

Step 7: Reflect on Your Lesson—Take time to review the lesson and think about what went especially well and why. Also give thought to what might be done differently next time or in future lessons. Most improvement in performance depends on self-development, so take time frequently for self-evaluation.

THE THREE BASIC SKILLS NEEDED BY SCHOOL PRINCIPALS

Katz (1974) identified three basic skills needed by effective leaders: technical skills, human skills, and conceptual skills. *Technical skills* assume an understanding of and proficiency in the methods, processes, procedures, and techniques of education. In noninstructional areas it also includes specific knowledge in finance, accounting, scheduling, purchasing, construction, and maintenance. The implementation of clinical supervision, to be discussed later in the chapter, would be indicative of a technical skill for an instructional supervisor. *Human skills* refer to the school principal's ability to work effectively with other people on a one-to-one basis and also in group settings. This skill requires considerable self-understanding and acceptance as well as appreciation, empathy, consideration of others, and other affective skill characteristics. Its knowledge base includes an understanding of and facility for adult motivation.

Conceptual skills include the school supervisor/principal's ability to see the school as an important part of the school district as a whole. This skill includes the effective mapping of interdependence for each of the components of the school as an organization, the educational program as an instructional system, and the functioning of the human organization. The development of conceptual skill relies heavily on a balanced emphasis of administrative theory, organizational and human behavior, and educational philosophy.

Perhaps one of the most common mistakes of practicing school principals is that of assuming that "I already have these skills. After all, I have been a school principal for several years." A leader must ask such questions as, "What would be the results of a school climate survey if completed by teachers, students, and parents in your school?" Such a survey would lend considerable feedback relative to your human skills if completed objectively. Have we become so inundated with testing scores that we neglect improving such phenomena as a positive learning climate in the schools? As noted by

Norton (2008), "Rather than attempting to initiate change and then realizing subsequent failure, school leaders should examine the school climate first and, if it is less than favorable, take steps to improve it before attempting program innovation" (p. 247). Climate improvement is discussed in detail later in this chapter.

You might ask yourself, "Do the faculty meetings in my school focus on such topics as professional collaboration, student learning theory, educational research results, curriculum results, or do the meetings consist primarily of news reports, scheduling matters, and other information that could easily be disseminated in a school newsletter?" To what extent do the faculty sessions focus on a discussion of technical skills related to teaching methods, learning styles, student engagement strategies, and other technical skills for increasing student learning in the classroom? To what extent do you as a learning leader possess a research posture? Are you a consumer, dispenser, and promoter of educational research as part of your instructional improvement responsibilities?

SUPERVISION STRATEGIES

Clinical supervision is not new to the scene of instructional improvement in education. Education borrowed the practice from the medical profession. Marzano, Frontier, and Livingston (2011) set forth an excellent brief history of supervision and evaluation in their book, *Effective Supervision*. As these authors note, "Few innovations in the field of education spread as quickly as clinical supervision" (p. 3). Reportedly, clinical supervision practices spread rapidly in education, and by 1980, an overwhelming majority of local school leaders were using the strategy for the improvement of teaching performance. As generally is the case, worthy concepts of positive practice in education move on; valuable aspect of practice remain in some form, whereas the less worthy aspects of the practice fall through the cracks of ever-changing education. The strategy of clinical supervision continues to be used effectively in many schools nationally.

For several reasons, the original concepts of clinical supervision, as a way for professionals to meet and converse about teaching concepts and methods that lead both the teacher and the supervisor to new heights of professional performance, lost support over time because it became a list of procedures rather than a positive interaction between a teacher and a supervisor to the benefit of both parties. For the purposes of this chapter and because of the possibilities of its effective results when properly conducted, clinical supervision concepts are discussed briefly in the following paragraphs.

Clinical supervision has the purpose of establishing a positive relationship between the teacher and the supervisor whether the supervisor is the school's assistant principal, principal, or other instructional supervisor. The practice is implemented with all members of the professional staff and not only for teachers who are not performing satisfactorily. Our observations have convinced us that great teachers are among the first to welcome the opportunity to be part of the practice. In fact, when organizations do not have a variety of growth opportunities available for their more effective teachers, they commonly seek positions in other settings.

A primary activity of clinical supervision is that of the teacher and the supervisor planning together. This might consist of the planning of a lesson, initiating a new unit, or considering the appropriate objectives for the time-span and student engagement strategies for the instruction of the new unit. Plans commonly include the specification of outcomes, anticipated problems, materials and resources, physical arrangements, student learning styles, and provisions for evaluating student learning. The teacher might ask about the supervisor's classroom observation plans and how best to record the actual instruction and events that took place during the lesson.

At the first opportunity following the observation, the teacher and supervisor get together and analyze the data relative to the observation. Both parties commonly perform this task separately before discussing it together. Were the agreed-on teaching strategies used and just how effective were they? For the most part, the supervisor is a listener during most of the post-conferencing. He or she asks appropriate questions that provide an opportunity for the teacher to implement self-evaluations. However, seldom or never does the supervisor suggest, "This is the way I would have presented that information." The supervisor points out the positive teaching moments relating to monitoring and adjusting the class presentation, teaching levels and providing for differences, teaching one major objective at a time, or using other recommended psychological principles of learning. However, personal judgments of poor teaching or "here is what I would have done" are avoided.

The post-conference is followed by a renewed planning meeting determined by both parties as being the most appropriate time. The emphasis is placed on planning a next lesson and the new objectives and appropriate changes that the teacher intends to employ. The supervisor might ask the teacher how we can plan the lesson so that we know if the students really understand or learned what they were supposed to be able to know and to do. The resumption of planning marks the initiation of the sequences of the clinical cycle.

The use of clinical supervision does provide information relative to certain instructional skills that should be addressed at in-service sessions with all teachers of the school. For example, it might be observed during the clinical process that teachers were not able to teach effectively to a stated objective or were not able to adjust a planned objective to the correct level of difficulty for students. Or, perhaps the inability to monitor and adjust the teaching by eliciting overt behavior of students, to check overt behavior, or to act on the interpretation given by students were common problems of teachers. To what extent were certain principles of learning such as active participation, anticipatory set, motivation, closure, practice, modeling, or reinforcement being used effectively in the classroom? Such data would be important for future inclusion in professional development services. Clinical supervision is a predecessor of mentoring and coaching that exemplify positive collaborative relationships between a supervisor and a teacher.

It is past the time when the school principal should be spending time on high-stakes testing. Rather, more attention has to be devoted to instruction in the classroom with additional time given to improvement procedures including models of clinical supervision, mentoring, and coaching. However, one does not automatically possess the needed knowledge and skills for these activities just by becoming a school principal. Each of these competencies must be sought, studied, and practiced. In addition, education continues to overlook the vital importance of such factors as school climate, teacher load, and mentoring as being of major importance for improving student achievement. We submit, for example, that attention to and improvement of school climate in the school will do as much or more for improving student achievement than any other activity that one might implement. These leadership needs are discussed in the following sections of the chapter.

PROFESSIONAL SUPERVISORY COMPETENCIES

One beneficial method of viewing the role of the local school instructional supervisor is to examine the primary tasks, competencies, and indicators of competencies related to the position. We commonly speak of this concept as competency-based leadership. "The term *competency* has its roots in the prefix *com,* meaning together, and the suffix *petere* meaning to aim at, to go toward, or to reach. Thus, the early use of the word meant to 'aim at together'" (Norton & Kelly, 2013, p. 29). A task is a major responsibility associated with a specific educational position. A competency is an ability or characteristic required for the accomplishment of the task at hand. An indicator of competency is a performance specification or overt behavior that provides a measurement of the individual's personal performance.

An example of a professional supervisory competency role is shown in table 6.1.

Table 6.1

TASK

1.0 To serve as the Instructional Leader for a high school program.

COMPETENCIES	INDICATORS OF COMPETENCIES
1.1 Ability to develop curriculum for the school's educational program	1.1.1 Sets instructional goals
	1.1.2 Designs instructional units
	1.1.3 Develops school curricula
2.1 Ability to provide instructional materials	2.1.1 Evaluates and selects learning materials
	2.1.2 Produces learning materials
	2.1.3 Evaluates the utilization of learning materials
3.1 Ability to plan for instructional staffing	3.1.1 Develops a staffing plan
	3.1.2 Advises in recruiting and hiring of school personnel
4.1 Ability to organize for instruction	4.1.1 Monitors curricular sequencing
	4.1.2 Cooperates in determining learning standards
	4.1.3 Helps teaching staff determine achievement goals
5.1 Ability to arrange for in-service education	5.1.1 Supervises in a clinical mode
	5.1.2 Plans with teacher in the development of individual development plans
	5.1.3 Serves as a mentor and coach
6.1 Ability to provide for classroom observations	6.1.1 Works with school principal in planning and conducting classroom observations
	6.1.2 Uses a clinical supervisory concept for teaching improvement
7.1 Ability to evaluate and assess instructional outcomes	7.1.1 Uses a variety of measures to determine the effectiveness of instruction in the school
	7.1.2 Uses the results of evaluation to assess needed changes/improvements
	7.1.3 Uses evaluation results to diagnose individual student learning interests and needs

A FOCUS ON THE POSITIVE RESULTS OF A POSITIVE SCHOOL CLIMATE

The factors of unsatisfactory student academic achievement and the inability to retain high-quality teacher personnel, according to early research findings, can be significantly improved by focusing on the improvement of the school's climate. "In the volumes of the research literature that presently exist, the conclusion is clear. Climate has a direct and highly influential relationship with the quality of student achievement in the school" (Norton, 2008, p. 63). Those schools with high-performance ratings also have positive school climates, whereas low-performing schools commonly have unhealthy climates that have been termed as being "toxic."

However, improving your school's climate cannot be accomplished overnight; rather the route to school climate improvement depends largely on the extent to which program, process, and material determinants are being assessed, programmed, and monitored by school personnel (Fox, 1973). *Program determinants* are present when the school is providing opportunities for active student learning, individualized performance expectations, varied learning environments, flexible curriculum and extracurricular activities, student involvement in rule decisions, and varied reward systems for personal academic and behavioral accomplishment on the part of all students.

Process determinants are effective when teachers and students are involved in the development of school goals and objectives. Effective communication is evident among school leaders, teachers, students, and parents, when accountability is closely related to the autonomy that teachers enjoy in relation to their classroom instruction and when there is positive evidence that the school's vision and mission statements are in place and operating.

Material determinants of school climate center on having adequate resources for instructional purposes, possessing an efficient logistical system that supports the programs of the local school. The school itself must reflect an environment for effective learning. Although it is beyond the scope of this chapter to discuss the full complement of school climate, we can recommend several excellent resources for further study of the topic. The book *The Principal as a Learning-Leader* (Norton & Kelly, 2013) includes a complete chapter on the development of a positive climate and learning culture in the school. The book *The Changing Landscape of School Leadership* (Norton, 2015b), discusses school climate as a major key for student academic success.

A third reference, *Teachers with the Magic: Great Teachers Change Students' Lives* (Norton, 2015a) discusses how high-quality teachers set the stage for engaging students in the learning process by addressing the individual interests and needs of the learner. For example, one "great" teacher was asked, "Why do you think that you are so effective in the classroom? How do you achieve this result?" The teacher responded as follows:

> I do not allow my students to fail. Successful learning is first and foremost. Student needs come as the priority. I do my best to deliver to individual student needs. It is a matter of trying and trying. The work is data driven. I constantly change assignments. Much time is spent on individual students. I work to know my students. Over time, I am able to build a safe climate based on trust. (Norton, 2015a, p. 110)

THE SEEMINGLY FORGOTTEN FACTOR OF TEACHER LOAD

In one of our visits with a high-performing school principal, he informed us that topics such as teacher load just do not come up anymore. Yet, we know that the workload of our best teachers can become such a burden that their teaching is virtually reduced to a level of actual mediocrity. Such a result is unconscionable. Overloading our best teachers not only reduces their effectiveness in the classroom but also is a primary factor in their decision to leave the profession. This chapter focuses on improving student learning through effective supervisory practices. Such conditions as school climate and teacher load have direct impacts on student achievement. To neglect these processes undermines the supervisor's ability to be as effective as he or she might be.

Give a moment's thought to the way in which a teacher's assignment is scheduled in most schools. As has been the common practice in schools today, elementary school teachers teach one grade level each day for approximately five to six hours. Supervision of the playground and lunchroom include at least another hour of work each day. At the middle and secondary school levels, most teachers teach four to five classes each day with at least one extracurricular assignment each semester. How different are these work assignments from those of fifty or more years ago?

When considering teacher load, the factor of class size dominates the discussion. Yet, class size is only one part of a teacher's total workload. The impact of class size on workload remains undecided except that some researchers have claimed that student learning is not affected positively by class size until it reaches a size of fifteen or fewer students (Glass & Smith, 1979). What percentage of teachers have only fifteen or fewer students? Yet teachers and others are more concerned about class size than any other load factor.

Would the number of classes taught each day, the different subjects taught by a teacher, or the nature of the specific subject taught make any difference in a teacher's workload? These factors certainly do make a difference, as do other factors such as the length of the school's class periods, the extracurricular assignments of the teacher, and the nature of the subject being taught. At the elementary school level, along with class size, factors such as the number of grades taught, preparation hours, and a combination of grades within one classroom makeup teacher load differences.

Research studies have revealed that some teachers have teacher loads greater than other teachers in the same school, three times greater! Yet their salary is not proportionately based on the load factor. Other studies have revealed that it is not uncommon for first- and second-year teachers to be carrying the heaviest teacher loads in any one school. Does such an arrangement seem fair and equitable or in the best interests of learners to you? Do you believe that you and other school principals are really aware of the total teacher loads each faculty member is carrying in the school?

Methods for determining equitable teacher workloads have been available for implementation for many years. Nevertheless, the use of these measures has been sparse to say the least. Is the workload of great teachers one reason for them leaving our profession in large numbers? We believe that we know the answer to that question, but why don't you ask this question in a teacher exit interview? If you take the time to learn how to calculate teacher load scientifically, you will do yourself, your staff, and your students a great favor.

A Look at a Teacher Load Formula

Find the teacher load units of a teacher who teaches two classes of English grade 11 (same preparation) and three classes of Social Studies grade 12 (same preparation). English classes have twenty-five and twenty-seven students and the social studies classes have thirty, twenty-seven, and twenty-three students. Each class is sixty minutes in length. The teacher's cooperative load (extracurricular) over the semester is equivalent to eight class periods per week.

Now before we illustrate the calculation of this teacher's total load, take a moment to guess the "weight" of this particular teacher load compared to teachers nationally. Is this teacher's load index average, below average or above average in your opinion? We will know the answer to that question after using the Douglass Teaching-Load Formula.

According to the Douglass (1951) formula:

$$TL = SGC\,[CP - DUP/10 + (NP - 25\,CP)/100]\,[(PL + 50)/100] + 0.6\,PC\,[(PL + 50)/100]$$

TL = units of teaching load per week;
CP = class periods spent in the classroom per week;

DUP = number of class periods spent per week in the classroom teaching classes for which the preparation is similar to that for some other classes;
NP = number of students in classes per week;
PC = number of periods per week in supervision of study hall, student activities, teachers' meetings, and other co-operations;
PL = gross length of class period in minutes;
SGC = subject grade coefficient (for English and Social Studies is 1.1);

$$TL = 1.1\ [25 - 15/10 + [(660 - 25\ (25))/100]\ [(50 + 50)/100]$$
$$+ (0.6\ (8)\ [(50 + 50)/100] = 31.515\ \text{load index}$$

In the foregoing example, the subject grade coefficient averages for eleventh-grade English and twelfth-grade Social Studies are 1.1. The subject grade coefficient for twelfth-grade mathematics, for example, is 1.0 and for twelfth-grade science is 1.1. The highest grade point coefficient for any subject is for agriculture, a grade point coefficient of 1.3.

Various states have established averages for teacher load indices in each subject area. The average for most every subject field is approximately 29.0 to 32.0. Thus, the total index load for the foregoing load problem, 31.515 is just about average for all English and social studies teachers. Using the Douglass Teaching-Load Formula for all teachers in your secondary school would give you valuable information on relative load inequities, equitable cooperative load assignments, and equitable teacher loads for teachers new to the profession and those teachers who were carrying excessive workloads. Such knowledge is not only beneficial for allocating work assignments, but also for many other purposes such as assigning students to classes, assessing load information relative to academic achievement results, and distributing extracurricular duties in an equitable manner. Although a teacher's class sizes might be reasonable, other load factors might place the teacher in the higher rank of excessive workload personnel.

The most reliable and valid teacher load formula available for your use at the elementary school level at this time is the Norton/Bria Teacher Load Formula (Norton & Bria, 1992). A major difference between the Douglass load formula and the Norton/Bria formula is the fact that the latter formula results in the total load hours and minutes spent by the teacher rather than resulting in a comparative load index for the Douglass formula. For additional information on calculating elementary teacher load, the reader can refer to Norton and Bria (1992).

To master the use of teacher load measurements, the principal will have to study the process in some detail. When this happens, other positive outcomes will soon evolve. Equitable teacher assignments will foster higher levels of job satisfaction. Personnel assignments will be far more equitable. Students will benefit academically. In addition, your implementation of the process will soon catch the interest of other administrative colleagues.

It is important that we understand that studying teacher load has the primary purpose of determining equity among the school's faculty. Research studies of teacher load have revealed that the workload of teachers in the school can be as much as 3:1. That is, a teacher with the highest load index can be as much as three times that of the teacher carrying the lightest load.

These inequities loom important for several reasons. It is logical for us to want an important task to be done by one of our most effective teachers. It is common for our most effective teachers to be most willing to go beyond the call of duty and so he or she accepts extra assignments without complaining. As a result, the excellent performance of the teacher can be reduced to a level of actual mediocrity.

The Walk-Through Classroom Observation

Reportedly, school principals are spending up to one-third of their time on the evaluation of teacher performance that includes classroom observations. Yet, there is limited evidence that this activity leads to significant improvement in student achievement. A walk-through classroom observation is recommended for several reasons. It is common for a walk-through observation to focus on one or more specific instructional criteria. Sometimes when describing an educational process indicating what it is not serves a good purpose. A walk-through is not an unannounced visit that comes as a surprise to the classroom teacher. Rather, it is a planned teacher–supervisor activity that evolves from the clinical supervision process or perhaps a mentoring session. It is not intended for use as a summative teacher performance evaluation; rather it is formative in nature and intended to help the teacher to assess some phase of his or her instructional methods. It is not an activity whereby the school principal gets to know the students; rather its single purpose is to help teachers help themselves.

Figure 6.1 shows the criteria commonly included on a walk-through checklist. In most cases, the supervisor simply has to check each entry as to whether it was evidenced during the walk-through observation or not. In most cases, a walk-through observation does not take more than five to ten minutes. A traditional teacher performance evaluation is more likely to take sixty minutes. The principal is able to do six walk-through observations in the same time that it takes to complete a formative classroom observation.

MENTORING AND COACHING FOR INSTRUCTIONAL IMPROVEMENT

We have contended previously that we support the implementation of the more effective professional activities of walk-through classroom observa-

---

Criteria Included in a Walk-Through Observation

Walk-Through Checklist

Check Each Entry Observed According to the Purpose(s) of the Walk-Through

Lesson Objectives
    Clearly Set Forth _____
    Shown on the Board and Discussed _____
    Key Ideas and Learnings to be Achieved _____

Introductory Set
    Lesson Tied to Previous Lesson(s) _____
    Learnings Tied to Life Applications _____
    Student Questions Solicited _____

Instructional Materials and Aids
    Materials & Aids Available and Utilized Effectively _____
    Audio _____
    Visual _____
    Tactile _____

Teaching Methods
    Individualization of Instruction Observed _____
    Adaptation to Learning Styles in Evidence _____
    Lecture _____
    Seat Work (individual) _____
    Seat Work (small groups) _____
    Questions & Answers _____
    Engagement Strategies _____
    Affective Characteristics (enthusiasm, humor, etc.) _____

Student Participation
    Student Engagement in Evidence _____
    Lesson Related to Student Interests in Evidence _____
    Lesson Related to Student Needs in Evidence _____
    Student Experiences/Questions in Evidence _____

Classroom Climate
    Healthy Classroom Climate in Evidence _____
    Respect for Students by Teacher Observed _____
    Student Relationships Observed as Positive _____
    Student Relationships Observed as Negative _____

Learning Assessments

    Variety of Student Learning Assessments in Evidence _____
    Adjustments in Lesson Plan Made if Necessary _____
    Question and Answer Techniques Used Effectively _____
    Lesson Closure Included Key Ideas Learned by Students _____
    Post-quiz or Other "Testing" Implemented _____

Additional Criteria

_____

_____

_____

Comments as appropriate for post-conference:

_____

_____

_____

_____

Figure 6.1 Criteria Included in a Walk-Through Observation

tions, climate improvement, and teacher–supervisor clinical supervision. The processes of mentoring and coaching hold many implications for improving teaching performance, cementing positive teacher–supervisor cooperative relationships, retaining quality teacher personnel, and improving student achievement. Additionally, a supervisor who is an effective mentor will foster improved instructional improvement as well.

"Mentoring generally refers to the art of helping to steer a subordinate or a colleague in the same field. Coaching, on the other hand, uses techniques for professionals or clients in a full range of backgrounds" (A. Allegra, personal communication, 2005). The coach helps the person to think through certain important questions relative to his or her development and then listens and sometimes helps the person with appropriate answers. For example, the coach might ask:

    What is it that we want this coaching session to achieve?
    What do we need to think about to achieve these results?
    What challenges or problems must be met to get under way?
    What opportunities are available to me now so that I can move ahead?

Such questions more than not will lead to more specific discussions relative to the person's career goals. The coach serves as a listener and a questioner that encourages thinking on the part of the client. The coach helps to discuss the purpose of the session and the problems that might need attention. Various options for resolving any inhibitors to a situation are discussed. The coach helps the individual consider best solutions or actions that should be taken and set forth follow-up procedures and timelines to accomplish desired ends.

A qualified mentor commonly follows a step-by-step procedure with his or her protégé. The mentor, rather than working with the protégé to resolve a personal problem or matters related to his or her teaching performance, uses problem analysis techniques to help clarify the problem and to determine the factors that appear to underscore the problem's existence.

When there is some agreement as to the nature of the situation being discussed, the mentor keeps in mind the individual's development plan in relation to its provisions and how it might reinforce the protégé's behavior or classroom performance. Just what has to be done to change the behavior that is inhibiting the teacher's performance? How can the protégé capitalize on his or her strengths to overcome or resolve the problems or meet the needs of improvement?

Phase three of the mentoring session must include the supporting of the collegial relationship that is required in any mentor–protégé relationship. The protégé is encouraged to place emphasis on his or her strengths. As previously discussed, working diligently to improve all weaknesses will most likely result in little improvement. As Clifton and Nelson (1992) note, people soar with their strengths.

We emphasize the fact that gifted teachers as well as marginal teachers can benefit immensely through effective mentoring by the school supervisor. Empirical evidence suggests that great teachers most often request such services. They welcome every opportunity to grow and develop.

Other instructional strategies can enhance learning for students by engaging them in the learning process. Such instructional activities as research projects, demonstrations, debates, seminars, interviews, cooperative learning activities, games, exhibits, role playing, specialists for teacher days, and case studies are among the strategies that great teachers report using to engage students in the learning process. For example, one math teacher had students "interview" several managers of their community's businesses and industries to determine how mathematics was used in their shops or companies. Another math teacher had students bring measuring instruments to school and demonstrate their uses in a brief oral demonstration. The wide variety of instruments commonly included micrometers and Vernier calipers, which gave additional opportunities for students to see the applications of decimal and common fractions. Each instrument was displayed on classroom bulletin boards in the classrooms accompanied by brief descriptions of its use.

This particular class project was written up and sent to the publisher of *The Arithmetic Teacher* for inclusion in this national journal. Two other instructional strategies are discussed in the following information. Our purpose here is to illustrate how the instructional supervisor can help the classroom teacher by using various student engagement strategies appropriately in his or her lesson planning.

Cooperative learning is recommended by instructional administrators and great teachers as well for enhancing student learning. "Cooperative learning involves structuring classes around small groups that work together in such a way that each group member's success is dependent on the group's success" (McDaris & Roseth, 2016, p. 1). These writers extend the definition of cooperative learning by indicating what it is not. Cooperative learning is not placing students in groups together simply to do their work assignments together. It is not having a group report on some topic whereby one student does the work and others just sign the report. Cooperative learning is not just putting students together to share or to just help one another; rather each student has a specific alternating responsibility as a researcher, recorder, report writer, discussion leader, or other problem-solving role as fits the case.

In cooperative learning, the teacher's role is changed. Sharan and Sharan (1976) suggest that the role of teacher changes from being the dispenser of knowledge to a guide and advisor of the group's learning process, a supervisor more than a presenter of information. The teacher serves to monitor each group's activities and assess the involvement and contributions of each student in the various groups. It is common for both the teacher and the individual group member to evaluate the group's success in meeting learning goals and completing the tasks of the assignment.

Specialists for teacher days have been used effectively whereby experts from various occupations assume the role of teacher for one day and teachers use that day for planned curriculum development planning. Such specialists might be managers from a leading department store, the chief engineer of a local telephone company, a bank manager, a judge from the city court, a hospital administrator, the museum director, school superintendent, major building contractor, manager of the city's electrical services, administrator of the welfare department, representative from the mayor's office, or other experts within the school community.

KEY IDEAS AND RECOMMENDATIONS

- The most productive supervisory results occur when time and effort are given to all teachers as opposed to spending the lion's share of the supervisor's time with teachers that are performing marginally or as unsatisfactory. Most improvements are realized when based on the teacher's strengths as opposed to his or her weaknesses.

- Effective supervisors give attention to strengthening their own technical, human, and conceptual skills. Conceptual skills focus on the realization that a local school is an integral part of the school system.
- The basic strategies of the effective supervisor are based on both affective and cognitive skills. Cooperation and collaboration are foremost in realizing the most effective supervisory results.
- Although teaching effectiveness is founded on the knowledge and skills of each individual teacher, such factors as school climate and teacher load are of great importance in the process of improving student academic achievement. Some authorities are of the opinion that one of the most direct ways to improve student academic performance is to improve the school's climate.
- Classroom teacher performance evaluations are certain to continue. Nevertheless, the implementation of such methods as walk-through observations based on supervisor–teacher cooperation and collaboration was recommended for their importance in the actual improvement of teaching performance.
- The titles and work responsibilities of supervisors and curriculum coordinators are both similar and different. Titles differ, responsibilities often differ, and work schedules differ depending on such factors as the school's student population and supervisory philosophy. Student achievement is the common purpose of both roles.
- Mentoring and coaching, although not new to educational practice, have proven to be more productive toward the improvement of teaching performance than mandated classroom teacher evaluations that tend to inhibit the more desirable characteristics of positive school climates, cooperation, and desired teacher–teacher and teacher–principal relationships.

Discussion

1. Consider the process of teacher performance evaluations. Requirements for evaluations commonly are determined by state laws. If you had the "power" to do so, what changes would you make in the requirements of current legislation in your state, if any? No changes? Defend your position set forth in your response on this matter.
2. The chapter content contends that spending the lion's share of a supervisor's time in an attempt to improve the weaknesses of low-performing teachers is unwise. The result commonly is to bring the performance of a "poor" teacher up only to a level of mediocrity. Take a pro or con position on this contention and set forth your arguments to support it.
3. You are meeting for the first time with your mathematics teachers to develop a curriculum guide for grades 7 to 9. Make a list of some

understandings and skills that might appear as objectives in the curriculum guide for mathematics. (Select a different subject area if you prefer.)
4. Do great teachers as opposed to new and marginal teachers really need to be supervised, mentored, and coached? Explain your response.
5. Instructional supervision must be implemented by those activities directly related to improvement of teaching and improved curriculum provisions that lead to student learning. How do such activities as clinical supervision, mentoring, and coaching serve the purposes of this definition?

CASE STUDY

Case 6.1: The Case of Questionable Competency

Delmar Erickson had served as a mathematics teacher for five years at Wymore Middle School. School principal Alberta Woolworth was in her first year at the school. She held a master's degree in education with a major in curriculum and supervision. In fact, Principal Woolworth had served as a teacher representative of English literature and composition on curriculum committees when serving as a classroom teacher.

Principal Woolworth implemented walk-through observations as a supervising procedure. She explained the procedure at the outset of the school year in a faculty meeting but had not as yet implemented specific instructional planning with individual teachers. She thought it best to get to know each teacher better before moving into any "clinical" improvement sessions.

Her first two walk-through observations of Delmar Erickson's math classes made it clear to her that he was a strict disciplinarian and was quite demanding of his students in regard to showing their work on math problem solutions and the mathematical rationale for performing specific math operations. For example, even though a student had arrived at the correct answer to a math problem, if he or she had not shown how the problem was solved with supporting math principles of unity, association, and distributive laws, the work of the student was rated unsatisfactory. Student grading in Erickson's math classes was "severe" as well; 50 percent of the students in his classes received a grade of D or F.

Reportedly, when one parent complained to Erickson about his "strict" expectations, Erickson replied, "Math is an exact science and that's the way I teach it." Then he just walked away.

Principal Woolworth decided to initiate individual teacher sessions to implement her clinical supervision methods. In her first meeting with Erickson, she opened the session by welcoming him to the cooperative instructional improvement activities and set forth the question of what ideas he had for focusing on improvement.

"What instructional areas might you have in mind that I observe during a follow-up walk-through observation?" she asked.

"I'm not certain that you are in a position to help me; that is, if I needed help," Erickson responded. "Is your major in the field of mathematics? I have been teaching the subject now for several years."

Discussion

Assume the role of Principal Woolworth and set forth in writing your response to him at this point in time. How might you address his question? To what extent would you be able to inform the teacher of a supervisor's role in the clinical process? What information from chapter 4 would be most helpful to you relative to your response at this time?

REFERENCES

Clifton, D. O., & Nelson, P. (1992). *Soar with your strengths.* New York, NY: Dell.

Douglass, H. R. (1951). The 1950 revision of the Douglass high school teaching load formula. *NASSP Bulletin, 35*, 13–24.

Glass, G. V., & Smith, M. L. (1979). Meta analysis of research on class size and achievement. *Education Evaluation and Policy Analysis, 1*(1), 2–16.

Katz, R. L. (1974, September). Skills of an effective administrator. *Harvard Business Review,* pp. 45–57.

Marzano, R. J., Frontier, T., & Livingston, D. (2011). A brief history of supervision. In *Effective supervision: Supporting the art and science of teaching.* Alexandria, VA: ASCD.

Milkova, S. (2016, February 2). *Strategies for effective lesson planning.* Center for Research on Learning and Teaching. Retrieved from http://www.crlt.umich.edu/gsis/p2--5.

Norton, M. S. (2008). *Human resources administration for educational leaders.* Thousand Oaks, CA: Sage.

Norton, M. S. (2015a). *Teachers with the magic: Great teachers change students' lives.* Lanham, MD: Roman & Littlefield.

Norton, M. S. (2015b). *The changing landscape of school leadership: Recalibrating the school principalship.* Lanham, MD: Rowman & Littlefield.

Norton, M. S., & Bria, R. (1992). Toward an equitable measure of elementary school teacher load. *Record in Educational Administration and Supervision, 13*(1), 62–66.

Norton, M. S., & Kelly, L. K. (2013). *The principal as a learning-leader: Motivating students by emphasizing achievement.* Lanham, MD: Rowman & Littlefield.

Chapter 7

Organizing for Curriculum Evaluation and Assessment

Primary chapter goal: To examine the related concepts of curriculum evaluation and assessment and the benefits related to student learning.

FOUR AREAS OF EDUCATIONAL EVALUATION

Four areas of educational evaluation have been identified: program evaluation, process evaluation, product evaluation, and personnel evaluation. *Program evaluation* centers on the evaluation of the design of school programs to determine if they meet, conceptually and structurally, the educational intentions of the planning individuals and groups. The desired answer is sought for the question, "Do we have the kind of program that we intended?"

Process evaluation focuses on information and data concerning the efficiency and effectiveness of the organization in delivering the services required by the program. Are there factors, for example, that inhibit the accomplishment of program goals? For example, are the "signals" received from the school district's office and the local school resulting in communication conflicts? Are constant changes in program requirements leading to ineffective program implementation?

Product(s) evaluation and *assessment* summarize the performance of school programs in terms of expectations. "Does the program work?" and "Are the desired outcomes being achieved?" "Are the 'involved personnel' truly committed to the program's goals and objectives?" *Product evaluation* gathers information relating to the performance of the school's program in terms of outcomes, standards, and expectations. Questions include "Does the program work?," "Are the desired outcomes being witnessed and if so in what specific ways?," and "Is the teaching curriculum in tune with the curriculum goals and objectives originally set forth?"

Personnel performance evaluations focus primarily on observing and collecting information regarding teacher performance. How are the system's personnel contributing to the planned programs of the school system? Assessment focuses on determining the effects of the evaluation data and the changes/improvements that appear to be required for personnel improvement. *Personnel evaluation* and *assessment* analyze the contributions of people in regard to the planned programs of the school. "Are personnel making a direct contribution to the planned program?"

Hard evaluation data as opposed to soft data are required for accountability. That is, rather than accepting soft data such as the number of personnel that completed an in-service program or the nature of the programs that were implemented to decrease student dropout rates, we ask, What were the results of the implemented programs? To what extent were student dropout rates decreased since the prevention program(s) were initiated?

All curricula to be effective must have an element of evaluation (Worthen & Sanders, 1987). The basic purposes of evaluation and assessment are to make clear the rationale of the program in question, collect information and data that serve to reveal the program's effectiveness, analyze the information and data and draw conclusions relative to the program's viability, make decisions for changes and/or improvements in the program in question, and assume the task of implementing the decisions relative to improving the program at hand. Thus, schoolwide evaluation, when purposely administered, gives school leaders beneficial information relating to the school district's and local schools' program designs, resources utility effectiveness, facilities usage, student achievement performance, implementation of policies and administrative regulations, staff development relevancy, teacher performance, and school community feedback.

When wisely administered, teacher testing in the classroom can serve the important purposes of diagnosing strengths and needs of program offerings, meeting school district and local school standards, student motivation, student success levels, and information related to student readiness and placement. On the other hand, overuse of high-stakes testing will result in numerous negative outcomes. We commonly speak of formative and summative evaluations in relation to teacher instructional performances.

A formative evaluation in this respect has the primary purposes of identifying the teacher's strengths and improving areas needing improvement. A summative performance evaluation is for the purposes of recommending the teacher for continued employment, determining if a specific plan for improvement is necessary, and determining tenure status or deciding meritorious rewards. Thus, formative evaluation is related to supervision that serves the purpose of continuous growth. Summative evaluations, on the other hand, do not focus on professional growth.

It is necessary to point out common misuses of tests, including misunderstanding a test score, inferring a "cause" from a test score, using only one test score for multiple purposes, having an inaccurate test description so that it does not do what the test implies, or having the presence of test bias. "Test bias is closely related to the issue of fairness—i.e., do the social implications of test results have consequences that unfairly advantage or disadvantage certain groups of students?" (Abbott, 2014, p. 1). That is, if students are not proficient in the English language or because of certain cultural customs the test is not fair to them. Three general categories of test bias were also identified by Abbott: construct–validity bias, content–validity bias, and predictive–validity bias.

Construct–validity bias is evident when a test does not measure what it purports to measure. *Content–validity bias* is present when its questions tend to be more difficult for members of one group of students than for other groups. Such bias might be caused by the fact that a test is more relative to one group's culture than another group's. A test is not *predictive–validity biased* if it predicts academic and test performance fairly for each group of students taking the test. As is the case with measurement error, some degree of bias is inevitable. This fact is one reason that authorities caution against using only one test score for making important policy decisions.

Abbott (2014) does us another favor by noting several ways to eliminate unfairness in student testing. Abbott's recommendations include:

- Striving for diversity in test-development staffing, and training test developers and scorers to be aware of cultural, linguistic, and socioeconomic bias.
- Having test materials reviewed by experts trained in identifying cultural bias and by representatives of culturally and linguistically diverse subgroups.
- Ensuring that norming processes and sample sizes used to develop norm-referenced tests are inclusive of student subgroups and large enough to constitute a representative sample.
- Eliminating items that produce the largest racial and cultural performance gaps and selecting items that produce the smallest gaps—a technique known as "the golden rule."
- Screening for and eliminating items, references, and terms that are more likely to be offensive to certain groups.
- Translating tests into a test taker's native language or using interpreters to translate test items.
- Including more "performance-based" items to limit the role that language and word-choice plays in test performance.

- Using multiple assessment measurements to determine academic achievement and progress, and avoiding the use of scores, in exclusion of other information, to make important decisions about students. (p. 3)

HIGH-STAKES TESTING

A study by Nichols, Glass, and Berliner (2005) revealed that a link between pressures associated with high-stakes testing and student achievement could not be established; rather the research suggested that increases in testing pressure related to increased retention in grade and dropout rates.

High-stakes testing is being questioned in most states today. The plea is for less testing and more time for classroom learning. Testing students on a perpetual basis is being faulted because empirical evidence points out that constant "drilling" of students has not resulted in student academic improvement. Rather such testing has added to the numbers of students being retained in grade, increased student dropout rates, decreased graduation rates, and increases in students that take the GED test. Questions related to the adequacy and validity of state tests have been expressed along with "inferred" reports that schools and states are using any and all means to avoid being labeled as underperforming schools. Of great importance are reports that the testing environment of today's classroom has resulted in an increased number of qualified teachers who leave the profession.

We submit that high-stakes testing violates the beneficial purposes of teacher testing. For example, the basic purposes of teacher testing center on the utilization of testing results for diagnostic purposes relative to the student's success level(s), the determining of student readiness for additional learning and possible placement, student motivation relative to visible progress and success, performance purposes relative to standards of achievement, and the teacher's curricular planning and lesson plan determination.

TEACHER TESTING

Supervisors and teachers must be knowledgeable and skilled in the administration of student testing and the purposes of various tests. *Norm-referenced tests* are best for maximizing differences in student academic performance. Such test results permit the teacher to determine how a student's performance compares to that of other students. Such information is helpful to the teacher when discussing a student's test performance in terms of stated standards set forth by the school district or teacher. *Criterion-referenced tests* show whether a student can perform a specific task. It is of help to the teacher and supervisor for showing the effects of classroom instruction.

Teacher-made tests perhaps are most commonly administered. Such test results are of benefit for diagnosis purposes regarding what instruction content has been learned and what needs to be reviewed and retested. In some cases, a teacher might use a pre-test to establish the status of the students' knowledge at one time and place. Most commonly, however, teacher tests are administered at the end of an instructional unit or end of a course. Such tests are given in many formats, including multiple choice, matching, essay, short-answer recall, and curriculum-embedded tests. Informal measures might include work samples, oral question-and-answer quizzes, seat-work observation, self-reporting strategies, and portfolio results. One teacher, on occasion, had her students write questions for inclusion in a class quiz. She was somewhat amazed just how relevant the questions submitted by students were to questions that were most important for the lesson at hand.

Student portfolios consist of a variety of work that a student has done over a period of time to accomplish learning objectives. Research reports, selected homework samples, written compositions, oral reports, test/quiz results, class notes, and other evidence that the student has met a required standard of accomplishment for an instructional unit or project are examples of what might be included in a student's portfolio.

Several benefits of student portfolios have been identified by Murphy (1997), Brown (1997), Zepeda and Mayers (2000), and others. For example, portfolio evidence can indicate a student's learning progress over an extended time period and can reveal the strength and needs including the need to return to important knowledge that most likely had been slighted in their student's learning, and therefore adjustments can be initiated. In addition, the content of students' portfolios can help the teacher assess the need for changes in his or her instructional lesson plans.

Other strategies of teacher testing include performance testing whereby students are involved in activities of problem solving, simulations, lesson summary feedback, role playing, and learning applications. For example, after a social studies teacher discusses the U.S. Constitution with emphasis on the Second Amendment, he or she might have teams of three or four students report on the significance of the amendment in America today.

Games also are strategies that can serve to engage in learning and serve as a testing strategy as well. In one example the teacher "invented" the game of Matcho based on the game of Bingo. During the math lessons of fractions, mixed fractions, decimals, and percent problems, Matcho cards were completed that included variations of these math numbers (e.g.,1/4, .75, 46%, 1 ⅓, and .5). If the fraction 1/4 were called and the student had that fraction on his or her Matcho card, they would place a marker on that number on the card. As is the case with Bingo, when a student had five numbers in a row on a card, the student would call out "Matcho!" However, the "test" came into play when the student had to tell how the fraction could be changed to its equal as a decimal or as a decimal fraction. When done correctly, the student would be named the winner. Such practices are attempts to make "tests" interesting and a positive learning activity as well.

Objective tests, essay tests, oral quizzes, debates, interest inventories, and chalkboard team competition are other ways that the teacher can test student learning and also evaluate the effectiveness of their own instruction. Most of these strategies not only test the learning levels of the students but also give the teacher important feedback on the effectiveness of the instruction. One teacher, on occasion, had the students themselves write a test question for a unit of the class subject. This teacher said with a smile on his face, "I can always be assured that a student will get at least one question right when I use this strategy."

EVALUATING AND ASSESSING SCHOOL CURRICULUM

Tyranny of the Textbook (Jobrack, 2011) included an excellent explanation of curriculum evaluation. "The curriculum, whether it is teacher or school created, or whether it is produced by educational publishers, rarely gets any attention. I suspect that this is because most people don't understand what it is or how to evaluate it. . . . Very few people, including teachers, administrators, and academics know how to evaluate curriculum" (p. 1). We have to agree with Jobrack's contention. Two of the main reasons for this dilemma are the facts that, first and foremost, administration preparation programs give little or no attention to this important task. Secondly, when curriculum requirements are established by agencies outside the local school setting, school leaders have become conditioned to accept the curriculum as it is required by the federal or state agencies.

Curriculum content and development historically have been controversial. Curriculum evaluation is controversial among some authorities as well. For example, Jobrack (2011) stipulates that "the full-time job of the school staff is to *deliver* curriculum, not to develop it" (p. 2). If we interpret this author's meaning to infer that teachers have no role in participating in curriculum purposes, design, and evaluation, we certainly cannot support his opinion. In fact, the foregoing quotation is directly contrary to the purposes of this book, that of local control of curriculum development at the school district and local school levels. Yet, we understand that local school leaders and teachers themselves do not feel competent in assuming leadership roles for curriculum practices.

We asked a small group of school principals just what they would do regarding curriculum development if indeed they were given the autonomy to do so. The general response given by members of the group was, "I don't know." This final chapter of this book centers on the topic of curriculum evaluation and assessment. We believe that the contents establish the groundwork for initiating curriculum evaluation and assessment at the local school district and local school level. The foregoing results seem to support Jobrack's contentions. Administrator preparation programs, state administrator associations, and local school improvement programs necessarily must give primary attention to preparing and improving personnel competencies in the area of curriculum and supervision administration.

Much more preparation needs to be done for school principals and other supervisors to become competent in curriculum development generally and curriculum evaluation specifically. Until measures are taken to bring curriculum development much closer to local school operations, by having school curriculum established by external agencies and mandated in such forms as core curriculum, present apathy and frustration among local schools will continue.

QUIZ ON CURRICULUM EVALUATION AND ASSESSMENT

The following quiz serves as an introduction piece for the discussion of evaluating the school curriculum. Do not just guess an answer; rather move to the next question. Check your responses with the correct answers at the end of the quiz.

1. Teachers, administrators, and those people who teach in higher education tend to evaluate curriculum much in the same way. True____ or False____
2. The rubric of content accuracy is the single focus of curriculum assessment. True____ or False____
3. Before evaluating any curriculum, the first thing to know is how much time is needed to complete the task. True____ or False____
4. To conduct an effective curriculum evaluation, the first step is to gather the test results for the particular subject area being assessed. True____ or False____
5. The primary purpose of curriculum evaluation is to determine if the curriculum accomplishes its goals. True____ or False____
6. The terms *evaluation* and *assessment* are synonymous. True____ or ____False
7. Which entry is a primary reason for evaluating the school's curriculum?

    a. To adjust the curriculum to meet the present knowledge and skills possessed by the school's faculty members

b. To help determine the effectiveness of the school's personnel hiring practices
c. To determine why students are not achieving the desired goals set in the curriculum
d. To determine how to adjust instruction so as to pass the testing program that the school or state requires

8. Which entry encompasses a primary curriculum evaluation model?

   a. Content, input, product, and process model (CIPP)
   b. Think, plan, develop, and perform model (TPDP)
   c. Test, evaluate, assess, and modify model
   d. Observe, evaluate, and assess model

9. Curriculum evaluation establishes

   a. specific strengths and weaknesses of a curriculum and its implementation
   b. critical information for strategic changes and policy decisions
   c. inputs needed for improved learning and teaching
   d. indicators for monitoring learning progress
   e. all of the choices listed
   f. only responses a and c

10. The primary questions to be answered before undertaking a curriculum evaluation are:

    a. What will it cost? How many people should participate, and how long will it take?
    b. Why evaluate? What is to be evaluated? On what basis will we evaluate?
    c. What test(s) will be used? Who will administer the tests? Are the tests normed?
    d. What qualifications will the evaluators possess? How long have the evaluators been in the school system? Are the evaluators high performing in their present school positions?

11. Which of the following entries are reasons for evaluating the school curriculum? (Check each entry that applies.)

    a. Improve teaching and better serve the interests and needs of students

b. Examine any effects of introducing a new curriculum
   c. Justify school program practices to the public
   d. Respond to dissatisfaction with school "program" procedures
   e. Settle conflicts within the school about power, roles, or personalities

Answers to the Pre-Quiz

Answers: 1. F; 2. F; 3. F; 4. F; 5. T; 6. F; 7. c; 8. a; 9. e; 10. b; 11. a, b, c, d, and e.

Your quiz rating:
11 correct: You can skip this final chapter. Nice job! You are not only on track, you could be the engineer.
10–9 correct: Very good work. You are right on track. You could be relief engineer.
8–7 correct: Good work. You could be the train's fireman.
6–5 correct: Not ready for engineering but you could be the conductor.
4–3 correct: Read the following quiz responses carefully while riding in the baggage car.
2–1 correct: Read the following quiz responses carefully while riding on the roof of the caboose.
0 correct: Better check the stop at the next station. You might be on the wrong train.

Discussion of the Quiz Results

1. "Teachers, administrators, and others who teach in higher education tend to evaluate curriculum much in the same way" is false. Because these groups and others commonly view curriculum differently, their ways of evaluating it differ. Some groups would contend that teachers should have no role in curriculum evaluation, whereas others indicate that teachers are in the best position to do what is necessary to evaluate it. Grade-level teachers' meetings can serve in the ongoing need for curriculum improvement. Discussions that center on the sharing of best practices, effective resources, testing outcomes, and learning achievement are effective ways to upgrade a curriculum guide and adjust program goals and objectives.

   Jobrack (2011) contends that teachers tend to evaluate curriculum as to whether materials will be easy to teach and whether students will have the ability to read and evaluate the content. On the other hand, academics consider accuracy as the primary test of curricular quality.

Administrators with whom we have visited commonly say that they evaluate curriculum in terms of such factors as its scope and sequence, value for helping teachers with lesson planning, and developmental student learning concepts.

2. "The rubric of content accuracy is the single focus of curriculum assessment" is false. Accuracy, of course, is of high importance for curriculum assessment, but there are numerous other rules or measures for evaluating the curriculum. Procedural steps commonly include the selection of a subject area and grade levels for the evaluation, collecting the data and information needed to assess the purposes of the evaluation, organizing the data and information, analyzing and assessing the data and information in relation to its relation to specific curricular purposes, reporting the information as appropriate to the case, implementing the stated procedures for additional study, and implementing recommended curricular changes or improvements.

Fink (1995) provides a direct response to the question of evaluating curriculum. The author simply states that the school gathers information about the quality of student learning that is taking place in courses and programs. Teachers then must make adjustments based on that information. Fink is of the view that, as educators, we need to know how teaching has affected student learning.

In the end, doing effective curricular evaluation requires the development of a research posture and finding in an objective manner the answers to such questions as, "How effective is our school's curriculum in meeting the interests and needs of student learners and improving the quality of individual student learning?"

3. "Before evaluating any curriculum, the first thing to know is how much time is needed to complete the task" is false. Perhaps the best answer to question 3 is set forth in answer 2. It recommends that the first step is that of determining the course or subject area to be evaluated. Of course, there are various models for curriculum evaluation that have been recommended by authorities. It is likely that the situation at hand will serve to determine what course or subject field should be evaluated at a specific time and place. For example, state or school board "mandates" might serve to answer this question. In other instances, teachers in a specific subject area might take the initiative in recommending the advisability of implementing a curricular evaluation. In any case curriculum is an ongoing and continuous necessity for school programs today. School leaders must become competent in performing that task.

As stated in an article by the Connecticut State Board of Education (2016), the answer to the question, "How will I know that my students know and are able to do what is expected of them?" is a question that holds an entire curriculum together (p. 6).

4. "To conduct an effective curriculum evaluation, the first step is to gather the test results for the particular subject area being assessed" is false. The first step according to most authorities is to consider and discuss the evaluation questions that must be answered and what specific components are to be considered in the process. Components refer to the subject areas, courses, grade levels, and content of the curriculum that will be the primary focus of the evaluation. Thus, the initial focus is on what is to be evaluated.

    Directly related to the initial focus of the evaluation are questions such as: What specific purposes will the evaluation serve? Are the purposes related to specific problems being encountered? Are the purposes related to scope and sequence problems? Are the purposes related to testing questions, such as unsatisfactory student performance results? How is the curriculum affecting student learning? What are the right questions that we want to answer?

5. "The primary purpose of curriculum evaluation is to determine if the curriculum accomplishes its goals" is true. A curriculum accomplishes this purpose by determining if the curriculum and teaching performances are resulting in positive student learning. Are established achievement standards being met and is the content of the courses being taught appropriate for meeting the interests and needs of all students?

6. The terms *evaluation* and *assessment* are different. Evaluation includes the methods that are used to collect information and data concerning such matters as student achievement, teacher performance, and curriculum effectiveness. *Assessment* includes those strategies that are used to analyze and diagnose the results or data collected from an evaluation. For example, an assessment might serve to determine how much students have learned or the merit of a certain curriculum program.

7. "A primary reason why a school should evaluate its curriculum is to determine why students are not achieving the required goals set in the curriculum," or choice c. In efforts to answer this question, competent administrative actions must be taken to reexamine the goals and objectives of the curriculum and then analyze, evaluate, and assess curricular contents for accuracy, scope, sequence, depth, timeliness, relevance, and quality.

8. "Which entry encompasses a primary curriculum evaluation model?" The answer is a, the content, input, product, and process model. Of course, you can find a variety of evaluation models set forth in the literature. Marsh and Willis (2003) discuss several models. For exam-

ple, these authors discuss evaluation models by Stufflebeam (1981), Tyler (1930), Stake (1967), Parlett and Hamilton (1972), and Eisner (1975). The content, input, product, process (CIPP) model is that of Stufflebeam. Content focuses on the environment in which the evaluation takes place. Input refers to the ingredients of the curriculum such as the goals, instructional strategies, the students, teachers, and required resources. The product component centers on goal accomplishments, and process is the plan of action that is pursued for accomplishing the curriculum evaluation.

9. Curriculum evaluation establishes all of the entries, or choice e. Thus, entries a, b, c, and d are correct responses. Evaluation of the curriculum when competently performed can identify strengths and weaknesses, give critical information for making strategic changes in curricular offerings, give clues to inputs/changes needed for improving teaching and learning, and identify implications for monitoring certain areas of curricular effectiveness. Models can and should be adjusted to meet the expectations of the evaluation team participants. Models provide steps to be followed and provide a logical way to begin the process and suggest important questions that should be considered in the pursuit of important information and hard data for analysis.

10. Three primary questions that must be answered before undertaking a curriculum evaluation are: Why evaluate? What is to be evaluated? On what basis will we evaluate?, or choice b. As noted by Marsh and Willis (2003), answers to these questions deal with policies and motives. Consider the implications involved in initiating a curricular evaluation for one of the following differing reasons: (1) to improve teaching and to better meet the needs of students; (2) to examine any effects of introducing a new curriculum; (3) to justify school practices to the public; (4) to respond to dissatisfaction with school procedures; (5) to settle conflicts within the school about power, roles, or personalities (p. 280).

Establishing the motivations for completing a curriculum evaluation determines in large part the primary purposes and strategies for its completion. What is to be evaluated commonly includes such components as the subject matter, scope and sequence relevance, teacher performance, student learning, and the surrounding environment status. Such information is relevant to determining on what basis to evaluate. For example, what value orientations will be in place? Is the evaluation to be formative as opposed to summative? Informal as opposed to formal? Internal or external? Or other philosophical orientations?

11. "Which of the following entries are reasons for evaluating the school curriculum? (Check each entry that applies.)": Answers a, b, c, d, and

e are all specific reasons for doing so. Our concerns, however, center on three administrative questions: Are the chapter contents plausible in view of the top-down practices of curriculum? Are school administrators prepared to implement the required curriculum practices? When will local function for curriculum development be implemented?

Preparation programs for educational leaders do not give high priority to the topics of curriculum development and contemporary federal mandates tend to require what curriculum is to be taught and also how to teach it. The rule is if there is no implementation of the mandated curriculum, no money will be received by the local school district. School vouchers increasingly are ways in which state and federal agencies are encroaching on public education. We submit that local control will only become a reality if public schools are kept public.

KEY IDEAS AND RECOMMENDATIONS

- Curriculum evaluation is essential for the purpose of assessing the school programs.
- A major deterrent to the implementation of curricular evaluation is the inhibiting factors of external mandates for curriculum provisions by state and federal agencies of government.
- A second inhibiting factor to effective curriculum evaluation is the lack of knowledge concerning the ways in which curriculum evaluation must be done.
- When effectively planned and implemented, curriculum evaluation holds many benefits for all those concerned: students, administrators, parents, and members of the school community.
- Unless curriculum autonomy is returned to the states and its people and, in turn, to the local schools, curriculum development and its evaluation will remain as "unfinished business."
- High-stakes testing presently is being questioned as a viable practice. If more local control is indeed given to the states and the local schools, opportunities for improved curricular practices will become available.
- Curriculum evaluation and curriculum assessment are different practices. Evaluation precedes assessment. First the evaluation process gathers relevant information and data relative to the outcomes of current curriculum provisions. In turn, curriculum assessment focuses on diagnosing the actual outcomes of present practices; the extent to which the curriculum is meeting program purposes. In brief, assessment considers the merits of the curriculum provisions.

- Many models have been established for the implementation of curriculum evaluation. The steps set forth in models serve as guidance for initiating the evaluation process, focusing on the purposes of the evaluation, and gathering relevant information and data. Most any model is conducive to modification to fit the purposes, needs, and environment of the school in question. Although there are several characteristics of importance for judging the effectiveness of a curriculum evaluation, content validity is first and foremost the most important single factor.

Discussion

1. If you are a teacher, give thought to the various ways that you evaluate students' learning in your classroom. List these practices specifically. After doing so, ask yourself about the reasons for using the practices listed. Which evaluation practices are implemented primarily because of mandated requirements and which are your own professional strategies? Which of the listed evaluation and assessment practices serve you best in regard to providing ways in which you might improve your instruction?
2. If you are a school principal, give thought to the evaluation and assessment practices in place in your school. Which practices are local in that these strategies are ones recommended by you and the teachers in your school? Which ones are most helpful in serving to improve teacher performance and student learning? If you had your own preference, which evaluation strategies would you continue to implement? Which ones would you most likely not use in the future?
3. Give consideration to the various evaluation strategies such as the use of student portfolios and others set forth in this chapter. Which of these strategies are in use presently in your school's classrooms? Which of these strategies might you consider for implementation in your school's classroom? Which strategies would you recommend for other colleagues?
4. Assume that you have been assigned as a mentor for a teacher new to your school. What ideas that you read and considered in this chapter might you share with your mentee?
5. This chapter centers on the importance of curriculum evaluation and assessment for improving student achievement. How are you presently incorporating such practices into your school administrative responsibilities?
6. How has the information in this chapter given you thoughts about your own responsibilities and opportunities to improve the curriculum in your school? What changes in present school practices and regulations

must be changed or just implemented for school leaders to improve curriculum evaluation practices?

CASE STUDY

Case 7.1

Ruben Lorenzo was in the first year as principal of Meadowlark Elementary School. Lorenzo had just received a master's degree in education with an emphasis on curriculum evaluation and supervision. Principal Lorenzo's final research requirement for the degree centered on the topic of curriculum evaluation and assessment. Because he was new to Meadowlark and was not completely familiar with the curriculum of the school, he thought it would be a great idea to implement a program of curriculum evaluation at this time.

At the first three meetings of the school faculty, Principal Lorenzo took ample time to discuss his research on curriculum development with an emphasis on its purposes. He noted that if the school was to improve teaching and learning the faculty had to gather information and data about the quality of student achievement in the school's classrooms and then take the necessary time to make decisions about the curriculum and adjust teaching in accordance with those findings. Lorenzo called the process Gather, Decide, and Adjust (GDA). GDA became the greeting sign when members of the faculty would meet and greet one another.

Gathering information and data became a time-consuming job of the schoolteacher. Testing, quizzing, and recording took priority for teacher activities. Testing and deciding began to consume more than 50 percent of the teacher's preparation time. It was not long before the faculty personnel began to use different words for the GDA slogan, none of which can be mentioned here.

Over time, GDA was consuming more than 50 percent of faculty meeting time. But what was of more importance, standardized test scores on the part of students failed to show any improvements in student learning. In fact, test achievement scores in most every subject area went down or tended to remain the same.

Toward the close of the school year, more complaints were being expressed by the teaching faculty and parents were entering complaints about the time being spent on questionable testing activities as opposed to classroom instruction. At the final faculty meeting of the school year, Principal Lorenzo addressed the group.

"Our GDA program is a correct one but the results have been much less than satisfactory. My research and experience have given me confidence that my program can work. So I do not plan to abandon the effort for next year. I do plan to adjust our slogan to GDADOE, which means Gather, Discuss,

Adjust, and Double Our Efforts. I hope that I have made this clear. Does anyone have anything to say at this time?"

Discussion

1. Assume that you are a teacher in attendance at the meeting described in the case. What would you most likely do at this time? Would you plan to stand and support the stand of principal Lorenzo or would you just remain quiet? What are the chances that you would stand and express your opinion as to why the GDA program is failing? Just how courageous might you be at this point in time?
2. Give serious thought to why principal Lorenzo's plan is not working. Set forth and elaborate on your reasons as to why the curriculum evaluation plan has not been successful.

REFERENCES

Abbott, S. (2014, August 26). *Hidden curriculum*. The glossary of education reform. Retrieved from http://edglossary.org/hidden-curriculum/.

Brown, B. L. (1997). *Portfolio assessment: Missing link in student evaluation*. ERIC Document Reproduction Service No. ED 414 447. Columbus, OH: ERIC.

Eisner, F. W. (1975). *Applying educational connoisseur-ship and criticism to educational settings*. Unpublished paper.

Fink, I. (1995). Evaluating your own teaching. In P. Seldin (Ed.), *Improving college teaching* (pp. 191–204). Bolton, MA: Anker Publishing.

Jobrack, B. (2011). *Tyranny of the textbook*. Lanham, MD: Rowman & Littlefield.

Marsh, C. J., & Willis, G. (2003). *Curriculum: Alternative approaches, ongoing issues*. Upper Saddle River, NJ: Merrill Prentice Hall.

Murphy, S. M. (1997). Designing portfolio assessment programs to enhance learning. *The Clearing House, 71*(2), 81–84.

Nichols, S. L., Glass, G. V., & Berliner, D. C. (2005, September). *High stakes testing and student achievement: Does accountability pressure increase student achievement?* Education Policy Research Unit. Tempe, AZ: Mary Lou Fulton Institute and Graduate School of Education.

Parlett, M., & Hamilton, D. (1972). *Evaluation as illumination: A new approach to the study of innovatory programs* (Occasional Paper No. 9). Edinburgh, UK: Centre for Research in the Educational Sciences/University of Edinburgh.

Stake, R. F. (1967). The countenance of education evaluation. *Teachers College Record, 68*(7), 523–540.

Stufflebeam, D. L. (1981). *Standards for educational evaluation of educational programs, projects, and materials*. New York, NY: McGraw-Hill.

Tyler, R. W. (1930). Measuring the ability to infer. *Educational Research Bulletin, 9*, 5–7.

Worthen, J. R., & Sanders, B. R. (1987). *Educational evaluation: Alternative approaches and practical guidelines*. New York, NY: Longman.

Zepeda, S. J., & Mayers, R. S. (2000). *Supervision and staff development in the block*. Larchmont, NY: Eye on Education.

Index

Abbott, S.: on learning standards, 69, 77, 78; on local control benefits, 16; on student testing unfairness, 137–138
academic performance, student retention and, 59–60
achievement results of students, principals accountability for, 3
achievement standards, for students, 2, 9, 18
administration, school: competencies, 12–13; dimension of, 12; scientific management concept, 6; twelve-month work schedule for, 5
Administration Industrielle et Generale (Fayol), 27
administrative leadership, 32–34, 70
administrative regulations, school superintendents drafting of, 2
administrative standards, for education supervisors, 82
administrators: as learning leaders, 9; Maslow's motivation theory for, 37; need deficiencies, 37; principal as human resources, 11
affective domain, of teaching and learning, 55–58, 56, 64
American Association for the Advancement of Science, 62
American Association of School Personnel Administration, 34

The Assistant Principal's Guide: New Strategies for New Responsibilities (Norton), 19, 82
assistant school principals, 17, 19, 41, 44
authoritative school superintendents, 7
autonomy, of teachers, 18

Barnard, Chester, 28, 34, 35
behavioral science movement, 34–35
Berkas, N., 90–91
Berlak, H., 1–2
Berliner, D. C., 9
Biddle, B. J., 9
Bloom, B. S., 51–52, 53
Bobbitt, John, 15, 29
body-kinesthetic intelligence, 55

CCSS. *See* Common Core State Standards
The Changing Landscape of School Leadership: Recalibrating the School Principalship (Norton), 19, 91
CIPP. *See* content, input, product, process
classroom physical setting, 61; colors, 62; noise, 62–63; Rendeiro on lighting in, 62; seating arrangements, 62
Clifton, D. O., 113–114, 129
clinical supervision models, 9, 118–120
co-curricular activities, 100–102
cognitive learning, 51, 61, 63; Bloom's taxonomy of, 51–52, 53; Piaget's constructivism, 52; situated cognition,

151

52–54, 64
color, learning influenced by, 62
Common Core curriculum, 77; example, 99–100, 101; principals disenchantment with, 90; states withdrawal from, 3
Common Core State Standards (CCSS), 27–28
competency, of teachers, 36, 112–113
competency-based education, 71
Competency-Based Leadership (Norton), 82
conceptual skills, of principal, 117
Constitution, U.S., on state authority for education programs, 1, 13, 18, 107
constructivism, of Piaget, 52
construct-validity bias, 137
content, input, product, process (CIPP) model, 146
content theories, 37
cooperative learning, 130
coordination, Follett on, 30
Course of Study requirements example, 79
Creative Experience (Follett), 30
creativity, mandated core curriculum inhibiting, 3, 13
criterion-referenced tests, 138
curricular developers, supervisor feedback to, 17
curriculum, 15, 89–109; case study, 20–22, 108–109; co-curriculum, 100–102; competent supervision for effective, 5–13; coordinator position description, 98–99; defined, 15, 18; goals statements and education objectives, 71, 94–95; key ideas and recommendations, 18–20, 107–108; McNeil on, 15; needs assessment, 97–98; overview of, 13–18; parents planning of, 45; PE programs violation of, 18; recommendations for 2016 and future, 25; standard-based high school, 99–100; statement of goals, 94; supervision dimension of, 12; traditional *versus* standard-based, 90–91, 107. *See also* local school curriculum; mandated core curriculum
curriculum development, 93, 106; of local school system guides, 95–96; model, 92; planning time for, 5, 89–90;

principles of, 44–45; public involvement, 11; specific aims and purposes, 92; statement of philosophy and aims, 92; teacher lack of right to, 16
curriculum evaluation and assessment, 135–150; case study, 149–150; CIPP model, 146; construct-validity bias, 137; education evaluation areas, 135–138; high-stakes testing, 138, 147; inhibiting factors for, 147; Jobrack on, 140–141, 143–144; key ideas and recommendations, 147–148; models of, 145–146, 148; motivations for, 146; personnel performance evaluations, 136; primary purpose of, 145; process evaluation, 135; product evaluation, 135–136; program evaluation, 135; teacher testing, 138–140
curriculum implementation, 8
curriculum mapping, 17, 97, 108
curriculum planning, 5, 45, 89–90

democratic supervision, 8
Dewey, John, 46, 49
Dickson, William, 31, 32
differentiated instruction, 104, 107
Dinsmore, K., 62
direct contact, Follett on, 30–31
division of labor, 26
Donahue v. Copiague, 16
Douglass Teacher Load Formula, 124–125

EAHCA. *See* Education for All Handicapped Children Act
education: competency- and outcomes-based, 71; Constitution on state authority for, 1, 13, 18, 107; curriculum goals and objectives, 94–95; evaluation areas, 135–138; free kindergarten through college, 11; parents engagement in, 5; practice efficiencies, 26; research negligence, 45; school boards on policy decisions, 16; scientific management concepts, 6. *See also* standard-based education
Educational Policy Commission, 92, 94
educational supervision: administrative standards for, 82; Constitution on, 1; curriculum development and, 1–3

Education for All Handicapped Children Act (EAHCA), of 1975, 81
Effective Supervision (Marzano, Frontier, and Livingston), 118
efficiency: Barnard on, 35; in education practice, 26; Gilbreth, F., and L., on, 29
ego development, situational, 50
equity, in standard-based education, 72
Every Student Succeeds Act, 4–5, 11, 16, 19, 90, 107
excellence, in standard-based education, 72
expectancy theory of motivation, of Vroom, 40

Fayol, Henri: POCCC management functions, 28; on scientific management, 27, 28
federal government: learning standards established by, 77, 78; local school curriculum control by, 2, 90; mandated core curriculum fund restrictions by, 1, 9, 18; No Child Left Behind Act and, 19, 90; student achievement standards, 2, 9
Follett, Mary Parker, 8, 19, 30, 30–31
Frontier, T., 118
The Functions of the Executive (Barnard), 34

games, teacher testing and, 139–140
Gantt, Henry, 27, 28, 29–30
general supervision, 114
Getzels, Jacob, 36, 38; social systems theory, 39
Gilbreth, Frank, 27, 29
Gilbreth, Lillian, 27, 29
Giles, E., 54, 55
goals, curriculum, 71, 94, 94–95
Guba, Egon, 36, 38; social systems theory, 39
Gulick, Luther, 27, 28–29

Haddermann, Margaret I.: on local control of schools, 14; on state and federal curriculum control, 2
Halpin, Andrew, 38, 39
Hanlon, J. M., 50–51, 51
Hawthorne effect, 31–32
Herzberg, Frederick, 35, 36, 38, 39

hierarchy of needs theory, of Maslow, 35–36, 37
high-stakes testing, 138, 147
human motivation, supervision concepts of, 38–39
human relations movement, 30–32; Follett and, 30–31; personnel services development, 34; Tead, Metcalf and, 30, 34
human resources administrator, principal as, 11
The Human Side of Enterprise (McGregor), 38
human skills, of principal, 117

individual curriculum program, 13
individual interests and needs, of students, 2–3, 13, 44
individualized learning standards, for students, 3
informal groups, in organization, 32, 46
instruction: differentiated, 104, 107; standards-referenced, 70; student adaptation of, 18; supervision dimension of, 12
instructional supervision: for classroom teaching improvement, 114, 114–116; lesson plans for, 116–117; of principal, 116; responsibilities of, 115
instructional supervisor, position description for, 42–44
integration concepts, of Follett, 31
intelligences: body-kinesthetic, 55; eight, 54–55; interpersonal, 55; intrapersonal, 55; logical-mathematical, 55; musical, 55; naturalistic, 55; research on, 64; theory of multiple, 54, 55; verbal-linguistic, 54; visual-spatial, 55
interpersonal intelligence, 55
Interstate School Leaders Licensure Consortium (ISLLC) Standards, 9
intrapersonal intelligence, 55
ISLLC. *See* Interstate School Leaders Licensure Consortium

Jobrack, B., 140–141, 143–144
job satisfaction, 35–36, 45; enriched motivating jobs, 36–37; Herzberg's two-factor theory of, 39

Katz, R. L., 117–118
Kelly, L. K., 19, 82, 104–106, 122
knowledge: principals bases for, 17–18; supervision bases of, 12–13

leadership preparation, for local school curriculum development, 5
learner-centered theories, 54; eight intelligences, 54–55; multiple intelligence theory, 54
learning, classroom noise influence on, 62–63
learning leaders: administrators as, 9; principal as, 10, 11
learning standards, 69–86; Abbott on, 69, 77, 78; administrative standards for, 82; Course of Study requirements example, 79; criticisms of, 77–78; examples of, 75–77; federal government establishment of, 77, 78; individualized for students, 3; key ideas and recommendations, 82–83; purpose, vision, mission and, 70–71; from school districts, 75–77; special needs learners, 81; standard-based education, 71–72; standards-based grading and student testing, 72–73; standards-based report cards, 73–74
Leger, Robert, 72–73
lesson plans, 116; Milkova on preparation steps for, 116–117
Lewin, Kurt, 8, 31
lighting, in classroom, 62
Livingston, D., 118
local control, of schools, 83; Abbott on benefits of, 16; Haddermann on, 14; increased parental involvement, 13; return to, 10; school leaders preparation for, 13; students interests and needs, 13, 16
local school curriculum, 3, 69; Every Student Succeeds Act for, 4–5, 11, 16; federal control of, 2, 90; Haddermann on federal and state control of, 2; leadership preparation for development of, 5; school boards implementation of, 17–18; school districts development of, 72, 108; state government control by, 2; for student individual interests and needs, 3
local schools: curriculum development of system guides, 95–96; instructional supervisor position description, 42–44; selectmen governing of, 6
logical-mathematical intelligence, 55

Management and the Worker (Roethlisberger and Dickson), 32
mandated core curriculum: Berlak on, 1–2; Common Core curriculum, 3, 77, 90, 99–100, 101; controversy over, 10; creativity inhibited by, 3, 13; federal fund restrictions for, 1, 9, 18; inhibiting factors, 3–4
mandated student testing, 10
The Manufactured Crisis: Myths Fraud, and the Attack on America's Public School (Berliner and Biddle), 9
Marzano, R. J., 118
Maslow, A. H.: hierarchy of needs theory, 35–36, 37; motivation theory for administrators, 37
material determinants, of school climate, 122
Mayo, Elton, 29–32
McConaughy, James L., 26
McGregor, Douglas, 35, 36, 38
McNeil, J. D., 15
mentoring and coaching, of teachers, 127–129, 131; cooperative learning, 130; specialists for teacher days, 130
merit pay system, 26
metacognition, 57, 58, 64
Metcalf, H. C., 30, 34
Milkova, S., 116–117
mission of school, 83; learning standards and, 70–71; statement examples, 90, 92–94
motivation, 35, 45; for curriculum evaluation and assessment, 146; Hanlon on situational ego development and, 50; Maslow's theory of, 37; supervision concepts of human motivation, 38–39
multiple intelligence theory, 54, 55
musical intelligence, 55

naturalistic intelligence, 55

need deficiencies, of administrators and teachers, 37
needs, students' individual interests and, 2–3, 13, 44
needs assessment, curriculum, 97–98
Nelson, P., 113–114, 129
No Child Left Behind Act, of 2001, 4, 8–9, 9, 19, 90, 107
noise, in classroom, 62–63
Norton, M. S., 18, 19, 82, 91, 104–106, 122
Norton/Bria Teacher Load Formula, 125

objectives, curriculum, 71, 94–95
organization: effectiveness, 45; informal groups influence on, 32, 46
Organizing for Work (Gantt), 29
outcomes-based education, 71

parents: curriculum planning, 45; education engagement by, 5; local schools involvement by, 13; on student retention, 60
Pattison, C., 90–91
PE. *See* physical education
peer tutoring, 60
performance: personnel evaluations on, 136; standards, in standard-based report cards, 74; student retention and academic, 59–60; testing, 139
personnel: growth development, 46; human services development, 34; performance evaluations, 136; specializations, 9
physical education (PE) programs, 18
Piaget, J., 52
Planning, Organization, Staffing, Directing, Coordinating, Reporting, and Budgeting (POSDCoRB) management tasks, 28–29
Planning, Organizing, Commanding, Coordinating, Controlling (POCCC) management functions, 28
policy-making responsibility, of school boards, 2
POSDCoRB. *See* Planning, Organization, Staffing, Directing, Coordinating, Reporting, and Budgeting

The Principal as a Learning Leader: Motivating Students by Emphasizing Achievement (Norton and Kelly), 19, 82, 104–106, 122
The Principal as Student Advocate (Norton), 82
principals, 7; accountability for students achievement results, 3; attention to theory, 45; classroom teaching improvement skills, 117–118; Common Core curriculum disenchantment, 90; conceptual skills, 117; curriculum development by, 5, 13, 19, 108; as effective supervisor, 11–12; as human resources administrator, 11; human skills, 117; instructional supervision by, 116; Katz on skills for, 117–118; knowledge bases of, 17–18; as learning leader, 9, 10, 11; as student advocate, 11
process determinants, of school climate, 122
process evaluation, 135
process theories, 37
product evaluation, 135–136
professional competencies, of supervision, 120, 123
Professional Learning Board, 62
program determinants, of school climate, 122
program evaluation, 135
public involvement, in curriculum development, 11
public school: curriculum development procedures of, 91–92; free kindergarten through college education, 11; original religious purpose, 11
purpose, learning standards and, 70–71, 83

Real Test of Education Comes Many Years Later (Leger), 72–73
religion, public school's original purpose of, 11
Rendeiro, M. F., 62
research: education negligence, 45; on student intelligences, 64
Roethlisberger, Fritz, 31, 32

scaffolding, 57, 64

schema theory, 52, 57–58
school boards: education policy decisions by, 16; elected community, 7; local curriculum implementation by, 17–18; policy-making responsibility, 2
school climate, 122, 122–123; material determinants, 122; process determinants, 122; program determinants, 122
school district level, supervision at, 41–44; position titles, 41; responsibilities, 41
school districts: learning standards from, 75–77; local control of curriculum development in, 72, 108; mission examples, 92–94; standard-based report cards adopted by, 73
schools: issues for, 11; mission of, 70–71, 83, 90, 92–94; purpose for students, 70. *See also* local schools
school superintendents: administrative regulations drafted by, 2; authoritative, 7; scientific management concept and, 6
scientific management concepts, 26; division of labor, 26; education practices efficiency, 26; Fayol on, 27, 28; Gantt on, 29–30; merit pay system, 26; POSDCoRB paradigm, 28–29; task system, 26; of Taylor, 6, 7, 19; terms used in, 26, 28; underperforming and, 26–27
seating arrangements, in classroom, 62
selectmen, local schools governed by, 6
semantic mapping, 58
Sergiovanni, T. J., 17, 51
situated cognition, 52–54, 64
skills: of principals, 117–118; supervision bases for, 12–13
Soar with Your Strengths (Clifton and Nelson), 113–114, 129
social systems theory, of Getzels and Guba, 39
specialists for teacher days, 130
special needs learners, 81
standard-based curriculum *versus* traditional, 90–91, 107
standard-based education, 71, 72; characteristics and benefits, 71–72; competency-based education and, 71; debate on, 69–70; excellence and equity in, 72; outcomes-based education and, 71
standards-based grading, 70, 72–73
standards-based high school curriculum, 99–100
standards-based report cards, 73, 83; benefits of, 73; problems with, 74; progress toward performance standards, 74; schools districts adoption of, 73
standardized testing, 4
State Board of Education, curriculum planning of, 89–90
state government: Constitution on education programs authority, 1, 13, 18, 107; Every Student Succeeds Act and, 4–5, 11, 16; local school curriculum control by, 2; student achievement standards, 2, 9
student advocate, principal as, 11
student failure, 59
student learning, 58–59; classroom physical phenomena on, 61–63; student retention myths, 59–60; student retention recommendations, 60–61
student portfolios, 139
student retention, 64, 83; academic performance and, 59–60; alternative instructional arrangements, 61; myths, 59–60; negative effects of, 59, 60; parents on, 60; recommendations, 60–61; team approach on, 60
students: achievement standards, 2, 9, 18; individual curriculum program for, 13; individual interests and needs of, 2–3, 13, 44; individualized learning standards, 3; Norton on instruction adapted to, 18; school purpose for, 70
student testing: Abbott on unfairness in, 137–138; high-stakes testing, 138, 147; mandated, 10; standards-based grading and, 72–73; standardized, 4
supervision, 5; dimensions of, 11–12; evolution of, 6; historical perspective of, 6–11; knowledge and skills bases for, 12–13; personnel growth and development through, 46; recommendations for 2016 and future, 25; at school district level, 41–44

Index

supervision, for classroom teaching improvement, 111–133; case study, 111–112, 132–133; general supervision, 114; instructional, 114, 114–116; key ideas and recommendations, 130–131; lesson plans, 116–117; mentoring and coaching for, 127–130, 131; positive school climate, 122–123; principals' skills, 117–118; professional supervisory competencies, 120, 123; *Soar with Your Strengths*, 113–114, 129; strategies for, 118–120; teacher load, 123–124; teaching competency, 36, 112–113

supervision, historical perspective: clinical supervision models, 9, 118–120; comprehensive programs for, 9; as curriculum implementation, 8; democratic, 8; elected community school boards, 7; ISLLC Standards, 9; mandated student testing, 10; 1900-1920, 7; 1920-1930, 7; 1930-1945, 7–8; 1945-1955, 8; 1955-1965, 8–9; 1965-1975, 9; 1975-1985, 9; 1985-1995, 9; 1995-2005, 9; 2005-2015, 10; 2015-present, 10–11; No Child Left Behind Act, 4, 8–9, 9, 19, 90, 107; personnel specializations, 9; principal as learning leader, 9, 10, 11; selectmen in colonial times, 6; student achievement standards, 9; teacher evaluations, 9, 10; teacher institutes and, 7; teacher turnover, 10

supervision and curriculum development, in America: administrative leadership, 32–34; administrator and teacher need deficiencies, 37; behavioral science movement, 34–35; case study, 47–48; concepts of human motivation, 38–39; curriculum development principles, 44–45; Gantt's scientific management ideas, 29–30; Gilbreth, F., and L., work productivity, 29; human relations movement, 30–32, 34; informal groups influence on organization, 32, 46; job satisfaction, 35–37, 39, 45; key ideas and recommendations, 45–46; recommendations for 2016 and future,

25; at school district level, 41–44; scientific management era, 26–29; Vroom's expectancy theory of motivation, 40

supervision concepts of human motivation, 38; Getzels and Guba's social systems theory, 39; Herberg's two-factor job satisfaction theory, 39; McGregor's theory behavior, 38

supervisor: administrative standards for, 82; curricular developers feedback from, 17; principal as effective, 11–12

task system, 26

Taylor, Frederick, 6, 7, 19

teacher institutes, 7

teacher load, 123–124; formulas, 124–126; inequities of, 126; walk-through classroom observation, 126, 131, 132

teacher-made tests, 139

teachers: attention to theory, 45; autonomy of, 18; competency, 36, 112–113; curriculum development right, 16; evaluations, 9, 10; Maslow's motivation theory for, 37; need deficiencies, 37; salary rewards for, 5; turnover, 10

Teachers with the Magic: Great Teachers Change Students' Lives (Norton), 122

teacher testing, 138; criterion-referenced tests, 138; games and, 139–140; performance testing, 139; student portfolios, 139; teacher-made tests, 139

teaching and learning, 49–66; in affective domain, 55–58, 56, 64; case study, 65–66; classroom physical phenomena, 61–63; cognitive learning, 51–54, 53, 61, 63, 64; Hanlon's Theorem 21, 50–51, 51; key ideas and recommendations, 63–64; learner-centered theories, 54–55; student learning, 58–61

teaching and learning tools, 57; metacognition, 57, 58, 64; scaffolding, 57, 64; schema theory, 52, 57–58; semantic mapping, 58

Tead, O., 30, 34

testing. *See* student testing; teacher testing

Theorem 21, of Hanlon, 50–51, 51

theories, 63; Dewey on, 46, 49; principals and teachers attention to, 45; process, 37; transformed into practice, 49–50. *See also specific theories*
Theory Y, of McGregor, 38
Tomlinson, C., 104
top-down curriculum mandates, 4, 10, 13, 18, 82
top-down management, 26
traditional curriculum *versus* standards-based, 90–91, 107
twelve-month work schedule, for school administration, 5
two-factor job satisfaction theory, of Herzberg, 39
Tyranny of the Textbook (Jobrack), 140–141

underperforming, 26–27
Urwick, Lyndall, 27, 28–29

verbal-linguistic intelligence, 54
viable theory, 50
vision of school, 83; administrators and, 70; learning standards and, 70–71; statement examples, 71
visual-spatial intelligence, 55
voucher system, 11
Vroom, Victor, 35, 37, 40

walk-through classroom observation, 126, 131, 132
Weber, Max, 27, 29
work productivity, 29

About the Author

Dr. M. Scott Norton, a former public school mathematics teacher, coordinator of curriculum, assistant superintendent, and superintendent of schools, served as professor and vice-chair of the Department of Educational Administration and Supervision at the University of Nebraska–Lincoln, later becoming professor and chair of the Department of Educational Administration and Policy Studies at Arizona State University, where he is currently professor emeritus. His primary graduate teaching areas include classes in human resources administration, school superintendency, school principalship, educational leadership, curriculum/instruction, the assistant school principal, and competency-based administration.

Norton is the author of college textbooks in the areas of human resources administration, the school superintendency, and competency-based leadership, and has co-authored other books on the school principal as a student advocate, the school principal as a learning leader, and administrative management. He has published widely in national journals in such areas as teacher retention, teacher load, retention of quality school principals, organizational climate, classified personnel in schools, employee assistance programs, distance education, gifted student programs, and others. Norton's publications include *The Principal as a Learning-Leader: Motivating Students by Emphasizing Achievement*, *Competency-Based Leadership: A Guide for High Performance in the Role of the School Principal*, *Teachers with the Magic: Great Teachers Change Students' Lives*, and *The Legal World of the School Principal*. Additionally, he has co-authored books, such as *Resources Allocation: Managing Money and People*, *The School Principal as a Human Resources Leader*, and *The Assistant Principal's Guide: New Strategies for New Responsibilities*.

He has received several state and national awards—such as the Arizona State University College of Education Dean's Award for excellence in service to the field and the distinguished service award from the Arizona Information Service—honoring his services and contributions to the field of educational administration from such organizations as the American Association of School Administrators, the University Council for Educational Administration, the Arizona Administrators Association, the Arizona Educational Research Association, and the President of the ASU College of Education Faculty Association. Most recently, Norton received a research grant from the Emeritus College at Arizona State University. The results of this research are reported in the aforementioned *The Legal World of the School Principal.*

Norton's state and national leadership positions have included service as executive director of the Nebraska Association of School Administrators, a member of the board of directors for the Nebraska Congress of Parents and Teachers, president of the Nebraska Council of Teachers of Mathematics, president of the Arizona School Administrators Higher Education Division, a member of the Arizona School Administrators Board of Directors, Staff Associate of the University Council for School Administrators, treasurer of the University Council for School Administrators, Nebraska State Representative for the National Association of Secondary School Principals, and a member of the board of editors for the American Association of School Public Relations.

www.ingramcontent.com/pod-product-compliance
Lightning Source LLC
Chambersburg PA
CBHW021844220426
43663CB00005B/395